BLONDE IN DEEP WATER

Brenda Fisher: The Story of a Channel Swimmer

North Wall Publishing

ISBN: 978-0-9568175-9-4

CPO Media www.mycpomedia.com

Foreword

By Peter John Winchester MBE

I have looked at many definitions of the word 'heroine' but none include the word 'friend'. I therefore consider myself unbelievably fortunate to be able to say that a born and bred Grimbarian heroine, Brenda Fisher, is my true friend.

This phenomenal lady, at the age of 23, won the coveted Daily Mail English Channel swim race, at the same time breaking the world record for the fastest woman to do so.

I was a child, and awe-struck at this wonderful lady's feat. At the age of 10, small boys are often smitten by outstanding sporting personalities - and Brenda Fisher did it for me! I remember listening at home on our crystal radio set to the reports of her exploit, and I was forever grateful to my father when he took me to the Rialto cinema to catch the Pathe News report.

I think it was aged seven, when jumping off the peanut barges moored at Grimsby's Riverhead, that I fell in love with swimming. So can you imagine how excited and proud I was, when on her return to Grimsby during her victory parade along Hope Street, I met this international celebrity?

In the summer of 1960, while training with the Grimsby Water Rats for an attempt at swimming across the River Humber, Brenda was sincerely inspirational with her advice and encouragement about open water swimming.

It was some years later when I realised my dream and successfully swam the Humber, but as soft as it may sound, I felt that Brenda was with me every stroke of the way.

I am humbled to be asked to write the foreword for this book, but at the same time I am inwardly exploding with admiration for a heroine I am fortunate enough, through the longevity of time, to be allowed to call my friend.

Portrait of Brenda

1

Enid Winship was a tailoress and lived in Hull when she met Albert Henry Fisher, a handsome chap from Hornsea. She may have only been a teenager at the time, but she knew this bright, determined and hard-working young man was the one for her.

Albert was born on August 11, 1889, the son of an engineer. At 5ft 10in tall, he had grey eyes and a pale complexion, tattooed with flowers on his arm and a woman's head.

Enid's parents, Mary Elliot and John Bradley Winship, were 23 and 24 respectively when they wed on August 3, 1878, at the Register Office in Cockermouth, Cumberland. Family tree research shows John was a bricklayer, and his father was Richard Winship, a gardener.

For young Albert, the sea had already called, as it did for many men of his generation. He began his seagoing career as a deckhand – his number, 11369, stayed with him for his entire career - and quickly rose through the ranks, becoming a skipper at the age of 21. Grimsby, at one time the world's premier port, was the obvious choice to make a home.

So the couple, happy and very much in love, married on June 18, 1913 in the Parish of St Paul's, Great Grimsby. His new wife, aged just 18, was to grow used to his absences. In 1912, he was certified as being entitled to act as master of any vessel connected to the United Navigation Committee of Grimsby. He skippered the War Wing in 1916, the Aphelion and the Pacific in 1917, and also the Fawn, Oceanie, Carmiavia, Calvia and Cavlamia. In his time, he also worked on the War Wing, Pacific, Leicester City, Leeds United, Huddersfield Town and Derby County.

On April 10, 1918, Albert was appointed as a skipper in the Royal Naval Reserve. This authorised - and required - him to repair on board and take charge as skipper any ship or vessel to which he was appointed by the Office of the Lord High Admiral.

He was awarded an MBE for his work during the Second World War, and was still fishing in1951.

"He was such a hard worker, providing for his family," says Brenda, fondly. "He fished in Greenland. It must have been a hard life. He never spoke about his time at sea when he was home. He was able to separate the two lives."

Once, he suffered a £150 loss after returning home to report that a mine had exploded in one of his trawl nets. He was at the helm of the Dunsby, belonging to the Boston Steam Fishing Co, when it was trawling the White Sea grounds. There was a "terrific explosion" on the sea bed and Albert told the local newspaper: "It almost lifted up out of the water. Fortunately it was too deep to damage the ship, but it blew to ribbons the net, floats and bobbins, all brand-new gear costing the best part of £150. We steamed back over the spot and there were thousands of dead fish floating about. Still, I don't mind them exploding on the sea bottom. My last mine was a year or two back and we lost the ship that time."

When he was not at sea, Albert and Enid ran a pub called The Empire, which was near where the yacht club in Grimsby is now.

Brenda with her parents

"Mother didn't like the pub," recalls Brenda. "When dad was at sea, she saw a house being built by well-known house builder Ernie Drayton, who was a friend of mum's before she met my dad. She bought the house while dad was at sea, in 1926, for £850, which was a lot of money in those days, and told him when he came home. She gave up the pub because it wasn't her cup of tea, so they left it and came to Windyridge, in Scartho Road, while dad continued his career at sea."

* * *

It was in a back bedroom at Windyridge where Brenda was born on June 9, 1927, the youngest of two boys and two girls. Guy was the first born, on November 8, 1921, earning the lifelong and affectionate nickname of Buster because he was a chubby baby.

Jessie, Brenda and Buster

Sister Jessie followed, then Foster, who tragically died at six months old of pneumonia, and lastly, Brenda.

Those formative years passed without further event, but when Brenda was nine-years-old, she was struck down by a case of sunstroke so severe that it left her paralysed down the left side. She was ill for a while, and was looked after by a nurse.

"I was very weak down my left side. I would sleep with my eye open and I had to wear special shoes for a while. A nurse looked after me in the back bedroom while I recovered. I have memories of mother talking about the illness, and I was ill during my birthday. It was just one of those things. I can see the nurse in my mind's eye now. She was ever so nice, and she stayed friends with the family for a long time. It was the only serious thing which happened to me in my childhood. Later, it was swimming and walking which built up my strength. Swimming became part of my recovery. The motion of moving my muscles in the water definitely helped. The only thing remaining of my illness is a weak left eye. I can't wink."

The family, determined that Brenda would not be hampered by her paralysis, focused on keeping her fit. "When I was in my early teens, we would go out for long walks on a Sunday, hiking with friends of the family all over the Wolds. Sometimes we went out in a bus and do a hike from whatever destination we'd chosen. We'd certainly get a few miles under our belts. It was a favourite pastime of Buster, Jessie and I - and Mac, our Scottie dog -

and a nice way to while away the hours together. We would pack up a nice lunch and find a rural nook or cranny to eat our sandwiches. Then we would

explore the nearest village, which were always so picturesque. We would cover miles. Buster would climb a tree… I loved being on the Wolds. It was - and still is - such a beautiful place. We were definitely a hardy bunch. I really like the winter, and even thick snowfall did not stop us from getting out and about. And Mac loved scampering about the countryside. He was such a robust little dog. He was my mum's really, but he loved coming out to play with us.

Brenda and Mac

"We went to the pictures a lot - everyone would go, mum and all of us - but walking was definitely our entertainment. We would regularly visit The Lyric, which was opposite where the Riverhead in Grimsby town centre is today. It was only a little place, just downstairs. There was a sweet shop at the side and we could all have sixpence to spend. I didn't really have any favourite film stars, but I remember seeing many,

many films. My best friend at the time was Barbara Eve, who used to live a few houses along. She was the same age as me and we went to school together; it was very handy living so close by! We were friends for many years and stayed in touch. Jean Cuthbert, who lived nearby, was another good pal. We had a nice bunch of friends. We all still send Christmas cards to each other."

* * *

Brenda was educated at Nunsthorpe Primary School until she was 14, and then went onto Oldham's to learn typing and shorthand.

Brenda in her school uniform

"I used to enjoy school and learning," Brenda says. "I was a prefect for about three years, and then became school captain. I wasn't very good at essays and I used to go out with the boy captain, Thomas Edwin Smith, so I would get him to help me. We met taking classes together, and would cycle together to school. He was a very handsome, quiet young man, and very nice to me. He was brought up nicely and was very respectful."

Mathematics was her favourite subject, and English and history her least. "My handwriting always was - and still is - awful," she confesses. "I have fond memories of Joan Capes, my PE teacher. She was lovely. You could ask her anything; she made going to school a joy."

Joan followed Brenda's swimming career long after she left school, and the former headmaster, Stephen Neal, wrote Brenda a congratulatory letter after one of her Channel swims, which she treasures to this day. Her prefect and captain badges are also carefully stored away, in an extensive and remarkable archive of her life.

* * *

Family connections and 'looking after their own' were very important principles to the Fishers. Brenda says: "I never met my maternal grandfather but my maternal grandmother, Mary, was very serious. She came to live with us at the end, and if she tapped on the floor, you'd have to go upstairs straight away. You would have to be seen and not heard when she was around.

"I was at school when she died. It was March 14, 1949. She was aged in her 90s, and we missed her."

Enid, Brenda's much-loved mother, died aged 81 in Grimsby's hospital, and donated her body to medical science in Sheffield. Brenda has arranged for the same, hoping her body can be of use once she has passed on.

"She was lovely, and a very good

Brenda's mother, Enid

mother," says Brenda, in tribute. "She was very kind and caring, and brought us up to be the same. I have some great photographs of her when she was young. She was really pretty, had glossy, auburn hair in two buns above her ears, and a good figure. My dad definitely got a good catch! She never left us. She was always home when we came back from school."

Albert died on March 4, 1958, aged 69. His obituary said he was an avid Grimsby Town fan, a keen angler and billiards player, and a member of the West End Bowling Club and the Grimsby Constitutional Club. A smoker, he passed away from a bad chest. Brenda is grateful he was there to see her 'glory days' of swimming.

Albert on a fishing boat

"I take after dad more than mum. Jess was more like mum. I was blonde, and dad was ever so blond. He was lovely. You never heard him swear and he never laid a finger on us - the threat alone was enough for us to behave.

"He would come home from sea and take me to play on the arcade games at Wonderland, on Cleethorpes seafront. He would be at sea for three weeks at a time, which feels long when you are a child, and then ashore for only three days or so. I remember missing him very much, and he missed us. I would go pick him up when the boats came in. I would wait, and dad loved it. He would come off the boat and give me a big, tight hug.

"He didn't drive but mum did. I only took him out once - never again though! I was lucky, because dad bought me a car when I was 17, as soon as I could drive. It was a light blue Hillman, and I was the envy of my friends. I ended up being a taxi driver most of the time.

"I remember when I first started to drive, mum and I went to the nearby Lincolnshire market town of Louth for the first time. The road near Louth back then was ever so narrow, and a bus came from the opposite direction. "I said to mum, 'What should I do?'. She said 'Stop', so we did and thankfully it squeezed through. There weren't that many cars on the roads then."

Brenda's parents, around 1915

The Fishers were a very sociable family. "My parents had many friends. They would socialise a lot, and played whist. We always had friends at the house; there were always people coming or going… our friends, my parents' friends, neighbours and relatives… it was very bustling and busy!

"Mum was always cooking. Sunday breakfast was an occasion - we would have the full works. It was delicious. The family liked fish and chips too. Dad would always cook it when we had people in. Every time he came in from sea, he would have baskets of fish with him. I'm sure they must have smelled, but we became used to it and never noticed."

In the Fisher household, with its three active youngsters, there was always something going on. In early 1947, the area experienced heavy snowfall. Albert got up one morning to find the front door open and the hall full of snow - as high as the table on which the telephone stood. It was such a drift he had to dig the telephone out. The culprit who left the door open was never discovered.

Brenda and Neddy the donkey

"Kirk's Farm was at the back of us. We'd go over the fence to visit. Jess and Buster liked riding the horses. I sat on one once, but I just didn't take to it. Neddy the donkey liked peaches and cream. We used to feed him, and found out what was his favourite by trial and error. He got out one night. A nearby house had beautiful tulips in the garden, and Neddy ate them all. He got told off!

"Mac was a lovely dog. He was spoilt and would get fed lots of things he shouldn't have, just like my pet does now. It was strange watching this area build up to what it is today. Back then, it was like living in the countryside - we were surrounded by fields."

* * *

So when did swimming start to become an important focal point in Brenda's Enid Blyton-style childhood? Following her almost life threatening paralysis, the family saw swimming as a way of building up her strength. It was a sport which already had the older Fisher siblings hooked.

Young Brenda at the bungalow in Mablethorpe

"We had a bungalow at Mablethorpe, where we would go on holidays, and it was there where I started swimming. It's almost as if I couldn't keep away from the sea," she says. "We used to love splashing about, and lots of our friends would come down - up to 25 at a weekend, squashed into that tiny place. Because we all loved swimming so much, in the end mother said we may as well have someone teaching us properly."

It was a decision which was to change Brenda's future.

2

Enter Herbert Cecil McNally - a popular swimming coach and former champion himself, known to all as Mr Mac. All three siblings began training with Mr Mac when Brenda was nine-years-old. It cost a guinea each for one private lesson.

"He was great," Brenda grins. "He was very jolly but strict - you had to do what he said. Sometimes I'd say, 'I want to go to the pictures', but I had to train instead."

Mr Mac, who lived at 16 Lovett Street, Cleethorpes, worked unloading ships at Immingham Docks. He was married with three sons and two daughters.

Mr Mac and Brenda

Burly and grey-haired, Leicester-born Mr Mac's greatest achievement was in 1906 when he was chosen to represent England in a water polo match against Belfast.

A former half-mile champion of the Midland Counties, he swam for the Leicester club for many years. He was also a member of the Leicester Life-Saving Team, which won second place in a national competition. After the First World War, he came to Cleethorpes and became involved with the Dolphins swimming club.

He was once a quarter-mile champion of the county and in 1936 he trained Haydn Taylor to swim the Channel. After training men and women from the Dolphins and Mermaids clubs, he gradually began concentrating on the Fishers.

"I would have to go into the dock and start swimming while he was still at work," Brenda recalls. "He would come over the bridge and watch to make sure I was doing what he had told me to do. Sometimes I used to cheat and wouldn't swim right up to the bridge. He didn't like that! I don't know how mum and dad found him. It's funny how people drop into your life and are meant to be.

"We started lessons with him after my paralysis, and I think he saw talent in me from that early age. He looked at us first and told us what he wanted - if we did it, then he would take us on. He made sure he wasn't wasting his time. You either do swimming or you don't."

* * *

Brenda, Jessie and Buster

Every Christmas Day, Buster would swim in the basin of Alexandra Dock, Grimsby, plunging into the icy cold water with nothing to keep him warm but a pair of trunks. He and his friends would emerge shivering, yet triumphant. The Christmas Day docks swim tradition is still continued today – one neither Brenda nor Jessie took part in.

"We would go and watch instead!" she chuckles. "You wouldn't have thought it of Buster really; when he was 12 he suffered from rheumatic fever and was weakened by it. I remember going to the docks, in the biting cold, and meeting at the pavilion which, years later, I would use while I was training. Now it's the site of the yacht club.

"A lot of people used to turn out to watch. There was always a fun, jolly atmosphere. Watching Buster, I never thought, 'I want to do that'. It always looked too cold!"

Brenda fondly recalls Buster's great friends, Ronnie Ireland, Eric Macklam and Terry Jackson, who would also brave the plunge. "Some girls went in; they were brave! The swim was only 50 yards - very short - but I never fancied it."

Buster was part of the Dolphins swimming club, while Brenda and Jess

Jessie and Buster after swimming the Humber

belonged to the Grimsby Mermaids, in which they would compete for years
to come.

"I can't say I was particularly inspired by anyone or anything when it came to
swimming - it was just what we did, as normal to us as going to the cinema.
Scores of us would go to the regular swimming galas held in Grimsby."

*   *   *

Jessie was just 15 and Buster 16 years old when they swam the River Humber
in 1938. Jessie crossed the estuary from Spurn Point to Cleethorpes in two
hours and 52 minutes. She made history by becoming the first female to
complete the crossing; an achievement as heroic today as it was then. And so
did Buster – by becoming the youngest male to successfully cross.

"There was no grand plan, but Buster and Jess wanted to swim the Humber,
so they did. I went on the boat.

"I didn't want to do it, I remember that clearly. I just wasn't interested. I was more interested in going to the cinema! I thought they were so brave, because it's a tough swim. The currents in the Humber are strong; dad always used to say they were the toughest currents more than anywhere. You have to be so strong to complete it. They were shivering when they came out of the water but very happy. It was amazing. I remember there being many people at the finish."

The Leeds Mercury reported the following day: "Mastering the tricky cross-currents of the Humber estuary, a 15-year-old Grimsby girl and her 16-year-old brother yesterday swam from Spurn Head to Cleethorpes beach – a feat no woman has previously accomplished, and which only four men swimmers of experience have done.

"They are Jessie, daughter of Skipper Albert Fisher, and her brother Guy. The distance is about six miles as the crow flies, but the swimmers covered a course of about eleven miles, taking advantage of the ebb and turn of the tide. They took to the water at Spurn shortly after 10.30 and waded ashore at

Swimming the Humber

Cleethorpes at 1.30, the official time for the crossing being two hours, fifty-two minutes.

"The progress of the boats which accompanied them was watched by crowds of holidaymakers on the beach and promenade at Cleethorpes, and as the swimmers came ashore, they were greeted with cheers. Jessie was hugged and kissed by many local swimming enthusiasts. She looked unbelievably fresh and unconcerned, and save that one eye was partly closed from the effect of salt water, showed no trace of fatigue."

"I don't feel really tired," she told the reporter. "I had a bit of trouble with salt water getting into my goggles through the swell beating in my face. It caused my eyes to smart, but when I got over that I felt fine. I just kept to the crawl all the way. I took refreshment once, some beef tea, when about half way over."

Buster, who was so fresh after the swim he could have done it again, said: "This was Jessie's swim. I only went to keep her company. We swam together almost stroke for stroke all the way. I am very proud of my sister. I think she is just about the finest girl swimmer of her age in the country."

The Grimsby Evening Telegraph reported: "Mr and Mrs Fisher are naturally very proud of their children – though 'children' hardly seems the right word to apply to young people whose physique has been so developed by swimming that they are veritable giants for their age.

"Their father had many anxious moments while sitting in the motor boat watching their progress, for the conditions were not of the best for such a feat. He seems to have been the only one of the trio, however, who had any doubt as to the result, for the two swimmers enjoyed every moment of it, and finished feeling fine.

"Jessie is still at school at Nunsthorpe. To achieve the Humber swim has long been her ambition. She is still not satisfied, and is already thinking of an even more difficult feat. Brother and sister are hoping to be the pioneers of swims which have not yet been attempted, although as yet they have no definite plans in view.

"Guy went to the same school as his sister, and when he left two years ago, he was head prefect. He is at present in the office of the Lincs Steam Trawlers' Mutual Insurance and Protection Co Ltd. One finds it difficult to believe that at the age of 12, he had an attack of rheumatic fever which left him with a supposedly weak heart, but such is the case.

"He has only been swimming seriously for about a year. The rare modesty with which this young man stands aside and gives his sister most of the credit for their joint achievement points to the particularly affectionate relationship between brother and sister. Mr and Mrs Fisher's youngest daughter, Brenda also gives indication of becoming a very good swimmer."

"Jess was excellent in the water," recalls Brenda. "She and Buster did distance swimming, while I did speed. They could endure long swims, and the training is very different for the two styles.

"It's to do with breathing and stamina. I had to swim for so many hours in the dock before I realised long distance swimming was my strength. Mr Mac would say, 'If you can do eight hours in the dock, then you're all right for the Channel'.

Portrait of the Fisher children

More high-profile swims were in store for Buster and Jessie, with Brenda in their wake. As they splashed about in the grey waters of the dock basin, the close-knit siblings had no idea how they would tackle nature together.

* * *

Tragically, Buster never saw Brenda complete any of her solo swimming challenges in later life – something he would no doubt have been immensely proud of. Buster was the perfect older brother, always looking out for his siblings.

"He was very protective," Brenda smiles. "He was a great practical joker. He was a pull-the-pigtails type of boy, but always stuck up for us. He used to work on Grimsby Docks before the war but went into the RAF as soon as he could.

"I was very young when war broke out. People changed and the environment seemed different. Wartime Grimsby was very different too. The blackouts were strange. We had a shelter built out the back, shared between us and two neighbouring houses, and spent lots of time down there.

"It was frightening sometimes, especially the noise of bombs dropping and aeroplanes going over. We had to carry our gas masks everywhere with us. We would play games in the shelter for hours. We were in there mostly at night, and I remember it being cold."

Buster, a former cadet, trained at Grimsby's Nautical School and underwent RAF training as a pilot-observer, completing his training in Canada and America. He did very well by coming second in his RAF grading examination, with a high percentage of 86 in navigation, maths and wireless.

"He didn't get much leave because he was abroad," she says, sadly. Brenda's face clouds slightly as she talks about the awful day the Fishers received a telegram.

It stated that Buster, airman 1238789, was missing. The telegram arrived on April 27, 1943 – Jessie's birthday. An un-credited newspaper clipping in one of Brenda's many scrapbooks reads: "The news that Sergt. Guy Fisher, a pilot in the RAF, is missing will come as a shock to many.

"Official news to that effect has been received by his parents, Mr and Mrs Albert Fisher, of Scartho Road. There are hopes that he may have

Buster in his RAF uniform

Brenda dancing

escaped with his life and all will hope for more reassuring news.

"Sgt Fisher was a well-known swimmer. He and his sister swam the Humber. He was one of the first cadets of the Grimsby (195) Squadron ATC." Buster never returned from what was only his second operational flight.

The news that, aged just 21, the brave pilot had been shot down and killed in action came through to Grimsby via the International Red Cross. He was buried at Meckenheim, near Bonn, Germany. Documents show he left £315 16s.

"Mum took it very badly," says Brenda. "She would never leave the house, especially during the time he was considered as missing in action. If he were still with us, I'm sure he'd be just the same old Buster. I like to think he would have been proud of me."

Recalling happier times, Brenda tells how she continued courting Thomas Smith after school, even becoming engaged at the age of 18.

Thomas, of Southfield Road, in Scartho, went into the RAF. He passed out of Halton RAF Training College and was stationed at Manby. They went their separate ways about two years later, as young people often do.

As a couple, they were keen competitive ballroom dancers; yet another string to young Brenda's bow. However, the discipline required the use of different muscle groups to that of swimming - and life in the water won.

Dancing was something she gave up gladly, but she still recalls the fun she had during lessons. "Bessie Reynolds, a neighbour from a few doors along, would teach us," she says. "During the war, we would clear the dining room of furniture and she would come in. Buster would join in too; that was before he joined the RAF.

"We were serious about dancing. I wouldn't say I was a competitive youngster but I always think if you are going to do something, you may as well do it properly."

It is a maxim which has stood her in good stead for her entire life.

*　*　*

When Brenda talks of Jessie, the admiration for her beloved older sister is evident. "Jess was lovely. She was a great sister and, because I was the baby of the family, she really looked after me. We did a lot of things together, not just swimming. We enjoyed spending time together and rarely fell out. She was very caring, and a dog lover too."

Jessie was born on April 27, 1923. She worked as a secretary, including for the local Conservative Association for a while, and at Scartho Post Office.

"She was an acrobat," Brenda grins. "She would get on the swing in our back garden and go upside down - and she was just like that in the water. She would do anything."

When Jessie married Bernard Robinson, she moved to nearby Holton-le-Clay – the first time the sisters had been apart. Bernard, of Legsby Avenue, Grimsby, was in the RAF. They wed at St Giles' Church, Scartho, where Jessie was given away by her father.

Resplendent in duck egg blue, she was adorned with white heather and burgundy accessories, carrying an ivory prayer book with blue ribbons and a spray of purple and white heather. The couple honeymooned in Morecambe, immediately after the reception. To make the journey, Jessie changed into a brown Scotch tweed coat over a green angora dress, with brown and green accessories.

Her former headmaster at Nunsthorpe School, Mr Neal, attended the reception at Scartho Church Hall, and revealed that the new bride's family had created a school record.

Jessie was head girl at the school when she attended, Buster - who could not attend the wedding because of his RAF duties - was head boy, and, at the time, lone bridesmaid Brenda was head girl.

Brenda wore dusky pink with navy blue accessories, carrying a bouquet of pink roses and carnations. Their cousin, George Owen, was best man, alongside groomsmen David Hobson, Eric Macklam and Leonard Brown.

The Grimsby Mermaids Swimming Club presented the bride with an inscribed clock. Overall, it was an out-and-out family affair, with Buster's absence noticeable.

Eight years passed before they started a family, having Sallyann in 1956 and Simon in 1962. Simon went on to have a daughter, Chloe; Brenda's great niece. She regularly visits Nana Brenda from home in Boston, in the south of Lincolnshire, spending hours playing with Brenda's dogs, the late Badger and his successor, Jester.

Brenda says: "Jessie would regularly holiday in a caravan at Chapel St Leonards through her adult life, still swimming. Aside from swimming, she was heavily involved in politics and for many years worked for the Conservative Party. She was elected to Holton-le-Clay Parish Council in 1982 and took an active interest in village affairs.

"It was 1992 when she resigned as councillor because she became unhappy in the position, but was still interested in what was happening. She was also a member of St Peter's Church, in the village. She passed away, sometime after her husband, on May 6, 1994, and a funeral service was held at Grimsby Crematorium on May 12. She was 71.

"I have very fond memories of her. She was such a good sister. She used to smoke a lot and I would try to get her to stop. She had a bad chest as a result, so that was partly to do with her passing on. But when all that came in, no one thought there was anything unhealthy in it. Jess started smoking from as soon as she could, when she was young. That was just the way of our generation, I suppose."

3

While a burning passion for swimming grew inside a young Brenda, she also harboured another desire – dancing. It was sparked in a back room of Windyridge by Ron and Betty Reynolds.

They ran a dance school above what was then Costellos, in Victoria Street, Grimsby. They would come and teach dancing to the entire Fisher family, when Brenda was in her very early teens.

"They were such good times, all of us having fun together as a family," she recalls. "We would clear the furniture to the side of the dining room so there was plenty of space, and have hours of fun."

Brenda soon displayed competence and quickly found partners to compete with. Unsurprisingly perhaps, she became an award winner, with titles such

Brenda (second left) with her fellow dancers

as British East Coast Dancing Championship winner under her belt.

One of her partners was Jack Broughton, who went into the Army. She also paired up with Bill Leckie, an airman at RAF Manby, and with partner Victor Naylor she would dance to the Big Band sound, quickly developing a talent for ballroom, including the waltz, foxtrot, quick step, tango and formation.

"Vic Naylor still rings me up now and asks me to go dancing," she says, laughing. "My first partner was older than me, a chap called Jack, who lived in Cleethorpes. I was a teenager then. He was in the Army and went to war. I don't know what happened to him after we parted ways. He was nice, and always walked me home to make sure I was safe. He was a real gentleman and a very good dancer. We were part of a formation team together.

"I also danced with Bill Leckie, but not for very long. When he came out of the RAF, he came to Grimsby to live and then went to sea, later going on to teach with Bessie Reynolds. We were really good friends.

"I danced with a few partners during the war, and then I was partnered up with Vic for some years."

Brenda receiving an award for her dancing

Brenda's costumes were made by a dressmaker, her favourite being a pale pink gown with netting. Looking back on those days with fondness, she says: "I liked Big Band music while I was growing up, and still do now. The dresses I wore were gorgeous, and I would wear very high heels. My mother made some of them, being as she used to be a tailoress, but I also had a dressmaker in Nottingham.

"Dancing in general was a very popular pastime, particularly during the war years. I would regularly go dancing at The Royal, in Cleethorpes. Dancing was very elegant and we always felt so glamorous. Sometimes, I'd compete away somewhere, come home on the train and go straight to work. I was very dedicated. We would go all over as part of the Reynolds' Royal School of Dancing, competing professionally."

She lists the famous local venue Café Dansant and The Assembly Rooms, in Lincoln, among the venues she performed at. She also recalls the annual Christine Orange contest in Lincoln. And awards included the Cleethorpes Chamber of Trade trophy… winning was in her nature.

Vic Naylor, a policeman, was her dance partner for years, until Brenda had to give up at the ripe old age of 22. "I had to stop dancing because it went against the training for my swimming," she recalls. "It worked different muscle groups and so on, and swimming won out in the end.

"Mr Mac said I should let it go, and I did enjoy swimming much more. I liked dancing and was sad at the time, but I knew I'd sooner be in the water. As soon as I made that decision, there was no hesitation."

* * *

Swimming became something which bonded the young Buster, Jessie and Brenda even closer together. Jessie had already made history in 1938 by powering her way across the Humber using only arm, leg and lung power to cut through the murky water. At 15-years-old, she had become the first female to cross the great divide.

Buster, just a year older, had joined her, and now they had the taste of success, they wanted more. In 1939, they tackled Morecambe Bay. The cross-bay swimming challenge takes place over ten miles of rough, open water, from Grange in the east to Morecambe in the west. Its history dates back to 1907, when the Morecambe Cross Bay Swimming Association was formed and the first race completed.

By the 1920s, six contests took place every year, and swimmers came from far and wide to participate. It was not unusual for the weather to be bad and waves to be huge, with many pulling out because the conditions were simply too adverse to proceed… in short, just the sort of thing to thrill the Fishers.

On August 21, 1939, the brother-and-sister team of Buster and Jessie made history yet again when both completed the Morecambe Cross-Bay Swim for the first time.

Sixteen-year-old Jessie's time of two hours, 51 minutes and 34 seconds was the fastest women's record in sixteen years. Buster did even better, finishing in two hours, 48 minutes and eight seconds – the best time for ten years and beating by ten minutes the record of Channel swimmer "Tornado" Blower, the Cross-Bay champion of four years.

Brenda and Buster

There were three competitors that day; the third was 50-year-old Charles Daly, of Manchester, who had swum the bay several times already. The trio entered the water at Grange-over-Sands at 3.40pm, half an hour after high water, in perfect weather conditions.

In a flat-calm sea with a slight heat haze, they swam strongly using front crawl and kept together for the first 30 minutes before Daly drew ahead. He gradually increased his lead until at one stage he was almost a mile ahead of the Fishers and kept to a regular 49 strokes a minute.

Buster gained slightly on his sister but was never more than 100 yards ahead of her. Daly still had an enormous lead when Morecambe came into sight, but met with a strong tidal current. As he battled with it, Buster and Jessie gradually gained on him. So great was the strength of the current that Daly was forced to take an oblique course and it was apparent he could not finish within the race boundaries.

When the Fishers met the current, it had considerably slackened and they were able to swim in a more direct line than Daly. Buster's pilot sounded for depth with his oar and shouted: "Stand up! You've done it!"

Buster stood and cheers went up from the pleasure boats watching at the finish. Three minutes later, Jessie joined her brother.

There were thousands of holidaymakers lining Morecambe Promenade, who greeted the swimmers with joy as they walked up the landing stage. Erstwhile Mr Mac, supporting the teenagers as always, was all smiles. The duo were "fresh and smiling after the swim", reported the Grimsby Evening Telegraph.

"After the swim, Jessie sat in her pilot boat eating lumps of sugar and her brother obligingly slipped back again into the water to pose for Press photographers."

In another edition it reported this little snippet: "Among the new words the war has given us and which look like becoming permanently included in the English vocabulary is 'blitzkrieg'.

"I have seen and heard it applied to many things and occurrences but never before, as it was the other night in Grimsby, to some swimmers. Mr F Dawson, secretary of the Grimsby and Cleethorpes Amateur Swimming Association, in the course of his annual report, commented that the epistle would hardly be complete without mention of Miss Jessie Fisher who, with her brother Guy, followed up last year's Spurn-Cleethorpes triumph with success in the popular Morecambe long distance swim.

"He said they seemed to have developed the week-end 'blitzkrieg' habit." It was not long before a question was on everyone's lips: "Will the Grimsby swimmers tackle the English Channel?"

Mr Mac confirmed that Morecambe was a precursor to the 'big one', and said he expected Buster and Jessie to be ready within two years. Mr Mac was instrumental in Cleethorpes dentist Haydn Taylor's Channel crossing, so it was only natural he would want the Fisher siblings to have a go too. The Second World War intervened, in the worst way possible, cutting Buster's life short. "We were all so strong in those days," Brenda recalls. "The media speculated for ages about Buster and Jessie possibly swimming the Channel. They were more than capable too. They both made a pact to swim the Channel together, and I have no doubt they would have done if Buster had not been killed. Jessie and I continued swimming after his death partly in his honour."

During the war years, Jessie joined the fire service. Brenda was still growing up, so time passed quickly for her. As usual, swimming was never far from their thoughts, even though they hardly swam at all during the war.

In 1946, Jessie, then aged 23, returned to the scene of a previous victory. She took on the might of Morecambe once more, and was the only woman to complete the course. She finished in four hours, eleven minutes and 55 seconds – the first to cross the bay since 1940. She went on to take five years out of swimming.

The Yorkshire Post reported: "Hauled out of the water, she remarked 'Well, that's that', put two cigarettes in her mouth at once to get the full flavour of a smoke, gulped down half a glass of rum and ate two hunks of gingerbread."

And this challenge was Brenda's first go at competitive long-distance swimming. Aged 19, she kept going for three hours and 35 minutes, but was advised to retire as the state of the tide made it almost impossible for her to reach the finishing line.

"I was in sight of the promenade," she recalls, "and I remember feeling so frustrated. But it really was a losing battle; the tide was just too strong for me. Jessie was brilliant. There were holidaymakers watching as the Mayor of Morecambe literally smothered Jessie with kisses as she was brought ashore."

"The sea was terribly rough in places and I was scared of being swept away from the pilot boat," Jessie told the Yorkshire Post. "Sometimes I was buffeted as far as 20 yards away by just one wave. The currents near the finishing point were awful. I never breathed properly for the last half-hour."

Journalist George Tansey, of The Daily Despatch, wrote: "Like the pleasant stranger who knows the short cut, the sands of Morecambe Bay are not to be trusted. They appear. They mislead. They disappear. They are a high road and, within an hour or two, a seabed.

"To walk over them between Morecambe and Grange, a distance of some nine miles, has required since the days of King John cool nerves and a skilled guide. To sail them when the flood tide sweeps back from the sea, a tough stomach and a skilled pilot.

"Most people wisely prefer just to look across them to the blue giants of the Lake District and the red glory of the sunset. But a few, a very few, attempt to swim them, while the fierce tide comes and goes. Which brings us to the gallant events of the week-end at Morecambe Bay."

He continued: "The sky was azure. The air was wine, the sea sparkled, the shifting sands were hidden. Near the shore, the sea caressed the feet of little children. A little farther out it gently, soothingly, rocked the red-sailed Morecambe luggers. All the cruelty and treachery of the sands were reversed for four brave swimmers, two girls and two men, who lowered themselves into the water nine miles away at Grange, and struck out boldly for fame and Morecambe pier."

This rather eloquent account, under the headline 'One Girl Conquers Sands and Tides of Morecambe Bay', has been kept among Brenda's many scrapbooks.

It gives an important eye-witness report of how rough the conditions were. The report continued: "The tide ran cold and strong, and it was roughish in the middle of the bay as the swimmers threshed on their drifting, slanting course. And the sands were waiting, biding their time. Minutes ticked into hours. The four little boats drifted apart. The tide turned to the ebb.

"Seemingly miles from land, the swimmers felt knees and fingers scrape incredibly on oozing sands. At last came the news that the cold tide and the shifting sands were winning the day. After two hours and 12 minutes in the water, the Londoner had given up. Severe cramp had finished him. The local man was brought ashore. He was cold and unsteady on his feet. He had found himself in barely three feet of water at times and had given up after three hours. That left the two girls. There was joking on the promenade. The women preened themselves. The men said women were 'better covered'. The fishermen identified the two little boats accompanying the Grimsby Mermaids - one drifting west but technically in a good position. One apparently better placed, but in fact beyond a sandbank. This second boat soon stopped. The glint of oar blades in the sunshine vanished.

"It was another triumph for the sands. After nearly four hours, Brenda Fisher had given up. Not that she couldn't have swum on, but she had no chance of beating the sands in time.

"Jessie Fisher was still left. The crowds raced west to meet her, but before they could get near, she had grounded in the sands - on the Morecambe shore. For a gloomy ten minutes, a report went round that she had been disqualified for landing beyond the westerly beacon, but it proved false. She had finally outwitted sands and tide and swum back in the shallows to land east of the beacon. She had conquered the bay in four hours, 11 minutes and 55 seconds. She looked fit and fresh.

"The crowd cheered. The woman Mayor kissed her. Then somebody observed that far from being two hours behind schedule, the great swim had finished at the best possible time after all. For everybody's lips were caked with salt, and it was turned 7.30."

In true Brenda style, she went out dancing that night.

A year later, Jessie conquered the bay again, crossing in three hours and 25 minutes, with Brenda in second, just five minutes later. Charles Daly, then 57, Eileen Fenton, Molly and Irene Farmer followed. The other competitors were forced to retire.

This time the sea was calm and warmer than on previous races, with a hot sun blazing down from a clear sky. But it wasn't all plain sailing. It took Jessie an hour to cover the final stretch, the shore in viewing distance. Witnesses said she was nearly in tears as she struggled against the ebb tide, doing little more than holding her own against it.

Jessie swimming Morcambe Bay

Brenda faced the same plight, swimming steadily but barely moving an inch. However, apart from a touch of sunburn, they made it. A warm bath to remove the grease and oil was required, and Brenda had no problems enjoying a dance at the pier that night.

The following day, all five girl swimmers went to the Swimming Stadium and spent some time messing about in the water, forgetting the trials of the previous day.

With them were 33 members of the Grimsby Mermaids Swimming Club, who had travelled to support the Fisher sisters. The Mayor and Mayoress of Grimsby, Alderman and Mrs J W Lancaster, also travelled to the bay to lend their support.

That year's contest was hailed as one of the most successful in its history. Back home, the sisters were presented with trophies at Grimsby Town Hall. Jack Mount, veteran chief pilot of the Cross Morecambe Bay Swimming Association, declared of Jessie: "I would like to see her in other years swim the Channel. I think she can do it. You have a swimmer of ability in Grimsby."

And the Mayor of Morecambe and Heysham, Councillor Willacy, said: "I have nothing but admiration for any lady who performs this magnificent feat. Anyone who beats the sandbanks and tides in Morecambe Bay is a swimmer of no mean ability."

Jessie responded by saying the presentation was a "great moment" in the lives of herself and Brenda, and wished Buster could have been there to see it.

In 1948, Brenda won the bay race. She finished in two hours and 37 minutes, the fastest for a woman in 34 years. The only female competitor among nine men, she swam the latter half of the route without goggles, as one of the glass eyes had fallen out.

Aged 21, she went into training for the 1949 swim at Eleanor Street Baths, wanting to shave off 17 minutes from her time. In the three months prior, she had given up competitive dancing - not an easy thing for the East Coast Pre-Amateur dancing champion of 1948, and the holder of the Christine Orange Slow Fox-Trot trophy.

But she happily moved on to hours-long stints in Alexandra Dock, all under the watchful eye of Mr Mac.

The 1949 race saw Brenda disqualified because the current swept her above the finish line. The following year, she decided not to take part.

"It's always a disappointment when something happens to make you retire, but it's just a fact of life," says Brenda. "You can't do anything to change the elements – it's humans versus nature, and humans never win! – so I just accepted it and carried on looking ahead instead."

By now, Brenda was a long-distance swimmer in her own right. It was only a matter of time before her older sister uttered the words: "Shall we try the Channel?"

4

Back in 1947, a young Irishman from Dublin made
a sea crossing of his own to England. Footballer
Christopher Patrick Johnston left his home to sign for
Middlesbrough FC, transferring to Grimsby Town in
1949. He made his debut on February 5, and he stayed
with the club until 1956, making 250 appearances and
scoring 16 goals.

Born in Dublin on July 16, 1924, Paddy, as he was
known to the general public, grew up to become
an excellent wing half. Later, the Irish international
would play for Skegness Town before retiring from
the game, but he wore his black and white Mariners
shirt with pride for some years.

Paddy Johnston

Considered as a senior member of the team, he turned down an opportunity
to take up a managerial post with Dundalk in the summer of 1953 because he
preferred to stay in Grimsby.

This preference could be largely put down to the fact that he had recently
become engaged to his beloved – a certain platinum blonde swimmer from
Grimsby called Miss Brenda Fisher.

"We met because Pat was lodging with Betty Schofield, a friend of mine," she
says. "I would visit, and he would be there. I remember thinking that he was
handsome. He was very easy to talk to, and that's basically how we started
courting."

They announced their engagement in February 1953 and the date for the
big day was set, to just over a year later. "Our courtship went so fast, looking
back," says Brenda. "We had lovely times together, and he was so supportive
of me and the swimming, even though he had his own career to think about.
It was an absolute joy spending time with him. Pat was a true gent."

Brenda with her father on her wedding day

There was snow on the ground when, on March 1, 1954, their wedding day arrived. The day dawned bright and crisp, and Brenda could barely contain her excitement.

It was a morning ceremony, at Corpus Christi, in Grimsby Road, Cleethorpes.

"When I awoke, I was very nervous but so happy," she says, flicking through photographs in a carefully kept album. "We married on a Monday to fit around Pat's training. My dress was blue and made of netting on top and satin underneath. My parents were proud, and I'm sure dad must have had some wise words for me in the car on the way to the church.

"Pat was Catholic and I wasn't. It was a nice service; it wasn't full of bells and candles, or things like that. The church was packed full of our families and friends. It was a bit nerve-wracking but I just kept focusing on Pat.

"I remember saying every word of the vows. I was so scared I was going to make a mistake, but I got through it. To be honest, it was quite a surreal experience and it was over before I knew it."

Two hundred well-wishers turned out at the church to watch the bride arrive just before 11am. Pausing at the entrance, she turned to see the admirers craning their necks for a view. There were so many people that policemen were holding them back. The church, decorated with hyacinths and daffodils, was waiting.

Brenda and Pat with their wedding party

Brenda wore a full-skirted ice blue dress of lace over taffeta and a sequined half hat with a shoulder-length veil. She carried an ivory prayer book with pink orchids and lilies of the valley.

The two senior attendants were Jessie and Pat's sister, Nellie, who wore smoky pink patterned brocade dresses with half hats of grey and matching gloves and shoes. Both carried ivory prayer books and red roses and lilies of the valley. The child attendants were friends of the bride, Susanne and Richard Macklam. Susanne wore lemon net over blue taffeta with a floral coronet, and held a Victorian posy of forget-me-nots, primroses and lilies of the valley. Richard was dressed in a white frilled blouse with long black velvet trousers.

Bill Leckie had the honour of being Pat's best man, and his groomsmen were fish merchant Eric Macklam and Ernest Munson. The service was conducted by Father C B Mitchell.

"Nellie has passed away now," says Brenda. "Pat had another sister and a brother, who was a farrier in America. My family loved him. We visited Dublin so I could meet his own family. His mother passed away before we married, but I met my father-in-law, Patrick, and Pat's siblings.

"When I walked up the aisle, I thought, 'I'm so happy to be marrying him'. He looked so handsome."

A reception for 300 people was held at the Winter Gardens, in Cleethorpes, and it was a whirlwind of a day.

"The cake had three tiers, and it was a proper, traditional wedding cake, complete with white icing. There was another cake with photographs of the Channel race on it in icing, as well as figurines of bathing belles and footballers in black and white strips.

"After the reception, we went straight to London. I wore a satinwood two-piece and a matching travelling coat and hat. We stayed for four days - and I had to go to a football match! I can't remember which match it was, but it must have been one of the big teams.

"We stayed at the Regent Palace Hotel, just off Leicester Square. It was very nice and the staff treated us very well. It was lovely to spend time with Pat, just us together on our own. Our lives were so busy, it was perfect to just be together. We visited Hyde Park for strolls, avoiding going for a swim in the Serpentine though!"

The couple's stay in the capital was short because they had to be back in Grimsby for Pat's footballing duties. "Really, we were both beholden to our schedules. We couldn't really go on holiday, but that didn't matter because we were both so passionate about what we did."

*   *   *

Supportive of each other no matter what, Brenda respected Paddy's commitments and he respected hers. That they were both keenly into sport simply helped matters along, but ironically, Pat did not like swimming. He nicknamed his wife "Hard Case", saying, very much tongue-in-cheek: "Who wants to stay in the water for 15 hours anyway?"

"He didn't like swimming," she chuckles. "I couldn't get him near a pool!"

They would go on very long walks together as part of Brenda's training, and she ardently supported Pat on the terraces at Blundell Park, the home of Grimsby Town.

"I played golf for a while," says Brenda. "It happened that I won a set of ladies clubs in a raffle and Pat, who was a very keen player, said I should try it. I had quite a few lessons but it just tapered off because, with golf, you have to be dedicated to it and I had other things in my life. Pat was a very good golfer and loved it.

"I never supported Grimsby Town before I met him, but after that my mother and I would go to every home match at Blundell Park. I was a regular sight in the crowd, and if anyone said anything bad or insulting about Pat, mother would tell them off.

"People would often say hello and talk to me, but I don't think they dare say anything about Pat, or his performance. I suppose I was the equivalent of the WAGs today! It's a different world. Footballers get paid so much these days. I don't watch it, but I was avid about it back then. I think Pat would have thought very little of today's footballers. He would probably have shaken his

Pat at the sweet shop

head a lot."

*   *   *

Not content with being a professional sporting couple, Brenda and Paddy also ran a sweet shop, which they bought from businessman Harry Betmead.
It was located in Grimsby Road, Cleethorpes, and took up a lot of their time.

"We'd be there at eight o'clock in the morning until at least six o'clock at night, and then I'd go training. I'd say to Mr Mac, 'Paddy and I want to go to the cinema tonight' and he would not let me unless I did an hour's worth of training first.

"There were never any compromises and, of course, Pat's training regime was strict too. He didn't smoke; he'd have a drink if he went in a pub, but he didn't drink as a rule. He was very healthy. It was good because he'd come walking with me. I had to walk for miles to aid my breathing in the water and he'd always accompany me.

"Grimsby was a pleasant place to live in at that time. At Blundell Park, there would be crowds and crowds, so much so that sometimes you couldn't get in. Luckily for me, I always got in. I've been in the ground when there were 30,000-plus gates. It was all standing then. I would be near the tunnel, so I could be where the players came out. Matches were an event. And if you made it to play for Grimsby Town, it was a big achievement."

*   *   *

Brenda and Pat enjoyed married life, until Pat passed away on May 25, 1971. "Pat was so fit and healthy," she reflects. "He always went golfing on a Friday evening, and came home not feeling very well. Mother suggested that he go to bed and rest. Over the weekend he really did not feel well at all, so we called for the doctor.

"He arrived at the house and examined Pat, and said he had double pneumonia. He was taken to Springfield Hospital and by the Wednesday, he had died. The doctor had no idea why he had developed pneumonia. He did think Pat had perhaps been kicked in the liver during football, but it remained a mystery really.

"By the end, he didn't recognise me. I hope he wasn't in pain. Bill Shankley sent me a lovely letter afterwards. I've been a widow now for more than 40 years. We did not have children – we had each other.

"If he were here now, he'd be on the terraces at Blundell Park and cheering at Grimsby Town's home games. He would also be playing golf, definitely. We spent some nice times together in his retirement from football. I still miss him now. I think he would have been proud that people remember my achievements."

Brenda and Mac

5

Captain Matthew Webb was the first person to be observed having successfully swum the English Channel, from Dover to Calais. It was 1875 and he finished in 21 hours and 45 minutes, a heroic time for a heroic man.

In his youth, he saved one of his brothers from drowning in the River Severn. Aged 12, he helped save a drowning comrade who fell overboard the training ship Conway, in the Mersey. And in 1874, he was awarded the first Stanhope Gold Medal by the Royal Humane Society, the highest award in existence for saving lives.

He had tried to save a seaman who had fallen overboard the Cunard steamship Russia during a gale in the mid-Atlantic. The young Matthew was picked up in a lifeboat after swimming for 35 minutes. The sea held no fear for him, so it was only fitting that he should have the distinction of the first man ever to cross the Channel.

To the Fisher family, Captain Webb had begun a challenge they were itching to attempt. In 1939, Buster and Jessie made a pact to swim the English Channel together.

The Second World War saw to it that Buster would never fulfil this dream. His death was a tragedy which shook the Fishers to the core, and even to this day, he is sorely missed. Knowing that Buster would want his sisters to carry on swimming, they continued to train hard, conquering Morecambe Bay and taking part in local galas.

So when the Daily Mail newspaper announced it was looking for willing participants in a race across the English Channel in 1951, Jessie jumped at the challenge.

"She suggested we should swim it together, and that was that," says Brenda. "We decided to send off an entry form. Mr Mac said to me, 'If your sister is going to do it, you might as well have a crack'.

"Jessie and I had to go all over the country to do tests in front of the selecting committee. We both passed and came back to Grimsby feeling very pleased about it all."

The sisters had been training since early January, including being put on a vegetarian diet and regularly swimming 500 lengths at a time at Eleanor Street Baths. There were 143 entrants from all over the world, and only 20 places. Both came through the tests triumphant, and afterwards they shared a plate of chips as a pick-me-up.

But fate had other plans for Jessie. She was suddenly taken into hospital with appendicitis and had to pull out.

"She was absolutely devastated, and so was I. We'd made a pact to swim the Channel together and now Jess couldn't. I was insistent that we both pulled out but she told me not to be silly and keep my place. I was reluctant but she promised that she'd support me all the way, and that I should do the swim for us both. That was persuasion enough."

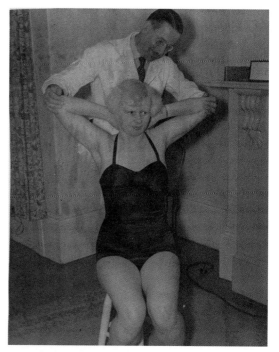

Brenda receiving physio

Alongside Brenda, Jessie had competed in a three-hour elimination test at Folkestone, only then revealing she was having an operation on her appendix. In fact, within half an hour of returning home to Grimsby the following day, she was in hospital. "Well you see," she explained to a local newspaper, "I was not going to miss my chance of being selected."

Jessie had travelled hundreds of miles to Folkestone only to discover she would need to perform a further six-hour test – scheduled for when she would be recuperating. In all, she needed two operations and could not race. But she kept her promise of being by Brenda's side during the swim – in the

42

support boat, at least, acting as her sister's manager.

In preparation for this final six-hour test, Brenda would swim for five or six-hour stints in Folkestone harbour, once being stung by a jellyfish. "No pain, no gain!" Brenda jokes, smiling at the memory.

* * *

Brenda was officially selected to take part in the Daily Mail international cross-Channel swim on June 25, receiving the news by telegram. Under Mr Mac's guidance, she embarked on a relentless and hard training programme.

"There was so much preparation," she says. "I used to train in the docks but it was very different from swimming in open water; totally different. It was horrible, in all honesty. Not only was the water shallow, but there were trolleys and all sorts dumped under there. I'd much rather swim in the Channel. It used to make me shudder!"

She once completed an eight-hour swim at Alexandra Dock, in Grimsby, covering 15 miles. "It is so monotonous in the water when you're just going round and round," Brenda recalls.

So to break the boredom, volunteers swam with her, including Jessie, while all the way through, crowds stood on Corporation Bridge to watch.
On the last lap, she sprinted 200 yards, ran up the jetty to her dressing room and dived into a tin of her mother's banana sandwiches. Sunday lunch that day had been two lots of eight sugar lumps and cocoa.

That night, she took a hot bath, fixed her hair and changed into a frock, ready for the Fisher family tradition of going into Cleethorpes on Sunday evenings in her bright blue Hillman.

Meanwhile, a group of Grimsby businessmen inaugurated a fund to cover Brenda's expenses. Within 24 hours of an appeal circular being distributed to more than 150 businesses and organisations in Grimsby and Cleethorpes, donations came in.

The first was 5s left by a window cleaner at Jessie's home in Beech Avenue. Chemist Tom Parker donated 4lb of lanolin, which cost £2 2s a pound, while regular massage and spine manipulation was given free by physiotherapist J Barnes Brown… There was no doubt about it; Grimsby was 100 per cent behind their blonde in deep water.

As the date of the epic swim drew near, Brenda travelled to Folkestone, in Kent, to continue her training before travelling by boat to Wissant in France. Jessie had been operated on and was recovering, and made the journey with Brenda – keeping her promise of supporting her all the way. Brenda was given a specially-made horseshoe in a floral bouquet by Folkestone restaurant owner Jim Heath, who was known in the area as the Channel swimmers' chum. They had made firm friends during her time in Folkestone and he singled her out for the honour. By now, she was ranked first favourite, with odds of 4-1, by London bookmakers.

Jessie, writing home, said: "Looking at things from a neutral point of view, after having seen 18 of the 20 competitors swimming since I have been here in Folkestone, my forecast is that Brenda has a very good chance of bringing fame and fortune to Grimsby."

And Mr Mac added: "I think that if Brenda can stick the distance, she has a good chance of proving that the confidence the committee placed in her was not misplaced."

* * *

It was Brenda's first attempt at swimming the English Channel, and her first trip to France. It was a rough crossing to Calais, with almost all of the competitors falling foul of seasickness. Brenda managed to hold out until

Brenda swimming the Channel

almost the end of the journey, but then succumbed.

And then the race was postponed because of bad weather. Brenda said at the time: "I don't like waiting but I am waiting to win for Grimsby. My money is lasting out all right but there is nothing I want to buy. I would like some nylons but there are only three shops here in Wissant, the butcher, the baker and the greengrocer, and they do not sell ladieswear."

In a message to her parents, she said: "You can rely on me. I shall see you as soon as I get across."

At one point, the weather was so bad that four swimmers – including Brenda – had to quickly come out of the water while training because of a dangerous offshore tide. In the meantime Wissant did its best for the anxious swimmers. A small café hotel, Des Bais, held an informal dance in between card games and reading books. Brenda partnered with Daily Mail man Sam Rockett, wearing brown with a sprig of good luck heather in her lapel and dancing to tunes of the day.

"It's a wonderful way to break the monotony," she told the Press. "The swimmers are grateful for the sympathy being shown by the French people. "It's a bit tiring but I am still confident and hopeful."

In the hotel, four miles from Cap Gris Nez, Brenda hardly slept a wink. Support, as always, came in the form of her sister. "I shall be in the water when Brenda needs me most – after 12 hours," Jessie told the Press.

Brenda was to wear her sister's Grimsby Mermaid Swimming Club badges, which Jessie wore during her big swims. Their mother had planned to wait on the English shore for the conclusion of the swim, but because the weather had postponed the start three times by now, she returned home.

"Now that I know Jessie will be with Brenda I am not worried," said Mrs Fisher. "I would like to listen in (on the radio) but I get very excited. I had to switch the Randolph Turpin fight off because of this but I think I shall have to listen to see how Brenda gets on."

When asked what her daughter would do if she won prize money, Mrs Fisher said: "She has not any idea. I doubt whether she has even thought about it.

"Probably she would just come home and not mention the subject."

Brenda enjoyed her first taste of France, but race day was the one thing on her mind. "We were called at 5am and were offered steak for breakfast," she says. "Fancy steaks at 5am! I couldn't eat a thing. We started off at 6 o'clock, and went to the beach in a bus."

The swimmers - who included eight who succeeded in the 1950 race - were taken to the sun-dappled beach off Cap Gris Nez. The sky was clear, the sea calm and the weather forecast for Dover was good. Each participant was provided with a private tent in which to smear on protective grease. While they did so, almost 3,000 French and British holidaymakers began wading knee-deep in the water to give the competitors a joyous send-off.

"It was a rush to get all greased up by 7am," Brenda recalls. "For half an hour, we posed for photographs and we were still being photographed when the starting gun was due to go off. Only the Egyptians were really ready for the gun to go. I had a mad rush down to the water. There was hopeless confusion.

Brenda greased up for her race

"My boat was pushing off without my trainer, but I told them to wait for him as he was collecting up my clothes. As it was, he left behind on the beach a coat, a mackintosh and a jacket to my best suit. I was rather upset about that. I also lost my handbag somewhere."

Brenda gestured goodbye, a small and restricted movement to preserve the grease protecting her body. On board the boat accompanying her were her mascots, a silver horseshoe, a box of heather and a blonde doll.

At 7.29am precisely on August 17, 1951, a green Very light soared into the bright sky over the French coast. Small boats bobbed on the waves and twenty of the world's most powerful swimmers plunged into the cold, calm waves towards England.

"The sea was calm and the weather was quite nice," Brenda remembers. "Myself and the rest of the swimmers were all lined up on the beach along with our accompanying boats. I was nervous because I'd never done anything like that before, but they shot the starting gun and we all just ploughed in. The first dive was a bit of a shock. I can still remember how cold it was. I got into the water and started swimming and suddenly noticed, to my horror, there was a great white boat coming right at me across my course.

"I was never so scared in my life. I could not see what to do and I was furious to think anyone could be so stupid as to steer a boat like that across a swimmer's path. I saw Jessie in a boat waving to me to go round, so I did, but I lost a valuable ten minutes through having to make such a wide detour. The boat did not touch me in any way but it was a nasty, aggravating ten minutes."

The greatest water race of endurance was finally on.

One minute passed, and the swimmers had struck off due west. Brenda suffered another mishap, when she was struck by the anchor chain of the control ship Ginasal. Thankfully she was not hurt. Later the Ginasal collided with a small launch, the Miss Thanet III, as it came alongside to collect cameramen's photographs.

At 8.15am, Brenda was third among the seven women competitors. At 8.50am, she fought Eileen Fenton for the women's lead and the pair held joint first place.

"I settled down to steady swimming and after two hours had my first feed of sugar lumps," Brenda recalls. "About an hour after that I became violently seasick, having been caught in the swell of a large boat which was passing. I felt very uncomfortable. In fact, I did not feel better until I had been sick again, some two hours later. That seemed to get rid of the trouble and after that, I was OK.

"It was most annoying because I had never been seasick before when swimming. I am a bad sailor but it was a strange experience to be ill in the water.

"Mr McNally had warned I might be but to take no notice and keep on swimming, so I just obeyed instructions. Another thing that might have made me sick was the petrol fumes from one of the organiser's boats that came to see how I was getting on.

"The petrol vapours from the exhaust lay on the water and formed an oily scum. I had to swim through some of that. The smell got right onto my tummy and it was most unpleasant."

By 11.30am, Brenda was following on the same route as the male competitor Roger Le Morvan. "I was fed at hourly intervals on sugar and chocolate. These feeds made a welcome break in the steady grind of crawl strokes. I never changed my stroke the whole of the way across, except when I was being fed. Then I trod water and did breast strokes"

For the men, it had become a battle between Egypt and France.

Egyptians Rehim, Arabi and Hamad were in the lead, but Frenchmen Morvan and Bombard were making a strong challenge.

Just before noon, Hamad was reported by his pilot boat to be just nine miles off the English coast.

For the women, Canadian mother-

Mr Mac in his boat

of-three Winnie Roach took the lead from Eileen Fenton, who was the first woman home in the 1950 race. But Brenda sprinted just before noon and caught up with Roach.

An announcement was made at the Dover headquarters of race sponsor the

Daily Mail at 12.45pm: among the women competitors, Brenda had officially taken the lead. Overall, she was in fifth.

"I was never told of the progress I was making, in any of the swims," she says. "I never thought about it really. All we wanted to do was get across. In this instance, what really spurred me on was knowing that Jessie was there too, and knowing how much she had wanted to do the swim herself."

It was around this time that the tide in the Channel changed and swept the competitors upstream. Although the race started in perfect weather, a wind of force was due to come from Ireland.

The pressure was on – to beat last year's record swim of 10 hours and 49 minutes, the winner would have to reach the English coast by 6.17pm. In the afternoon, the swimmers formed into two large groups, one to the east and one to the west.

At the head of the western group was Egyptian Hamad, with his fellow countrymen Rehim and Arabi behind in that order. In fourth was Englishman Godfrey Chapman, from Weymouth. The 21-year-old was the baby of the race, and was doing well. In the eastern group, Frenchman Le Morvan was in the lead.

At 3pm, Brenda was just eight miles from South Foreland, followed by Roach, Fenton and Jenny James – and it was reported that she was challenging the men for overall leadership of the race. Sam Rockett, the Daily Mail's training supervisor, said: "Brenda's performance is the one big surprise of the race."

A media report filed from Brenda's support boat read: "She is swimming strongly and putting up a tremendous performance.

Brenda after her Channel swim

Though she is well within sight of land, she is now approaching the most difficult part of her task. She will meet the strong currents that sweep down between the mainland and the Goodwins.

"This will be her great test, for it is here and for this reason that so many swimmers have failed.

"But Brenda is in great trim. Her trainer, Mr McNally, whose pipe is alight and blowing furiously, which means that everything is going well, said, 'She is putting up a remarkable performance, and is swimming better than ever'.

"The 23-years-old Grimsby girl had so far had a chapter of accidents but was putting up a gallant fight. She had trouble with her goggles, which kept slipping, and an attack of sea sickness, neither of which gave her a very encouraging start.

"She later settled down and three hours after the start, while she was taking food, she said to her companions in the boat, 'Don't worry, I am feeling fine.'" Lumps of sugar, sweet tea and just one square of chocolate was all she could take to sustain her body.

"What did I think about? Oh, my family, all those near and dear to me, my job, a thousand and one things," she told journalists, safe and sound on dry land at Folkestone. "One thing I did not do. I did not count my strokes. I had done that on previous big swims, but this time I decided not to.

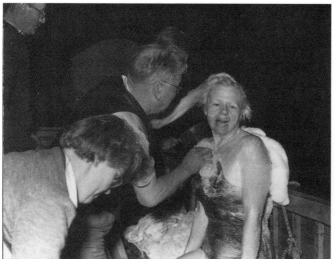

"I thought how much I owed to my pilot. I had been lucky to get Mr Jim Atkins, a fisherman and lobsterman, of St Margaret's Bay. He rowed every inch of the course and never left his compass for a second. It was largely due to him that I did so well. I know he got

Brenda having a rub down

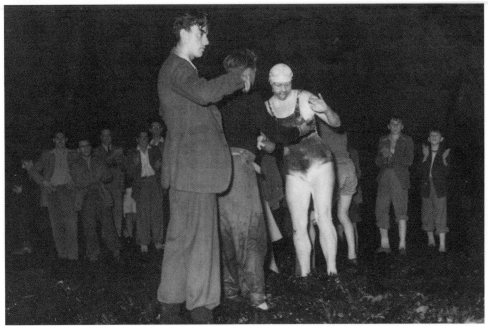

a great kick out of it. I was the first woman he had ever piloted in a Channel swim and he certainly did his best for me. His assistant, Charlie, was a great help too.

"What made all the difference to me, and I think to all the other swimmers, was starting and finishing the race in daylight. I was dreading having to come in in the dark, but I need not have worried as it turned out.

"While I was swimming, I would watch Mr McNally's pipe. When he puffed, I knew I was all right; when he began to fidget and fumble for matches, he was concerned about time and tide.

"He did not know it at the time, but the sight of that pipe smoking madly was my greatest comfort."

Meanwhile, Jessie, in the support boat, did count Brenda's stroke – twenty-five every minute. This increased to thirty as she neared home. On her way over, they saw several large vessels, including the regular cross-Channel steamer making for Dover.

"What delighted us all was the behaviour of a coast collier when we were nearing the shore," Brenda told the Press. "The collier was heading straight for me but the people in my boat, realising the danger, stood up and made frantic signals for it to go seaward of me, and the collier answered by going at least two and a half miles off course.

"As it passed me, it gave a hearty toot on its siren. I was given a great cheer, too, by the passengers on a pleasure boat from Ramsgate. They all crowded to the side and gave me a wonderful greeting."

Land was in sight. In fact, Brenda could practically feel it underneath her feet. She recalls: "When I first saw the coastline of England, I was ecstatic. Mr Mac said, 'Forget about it for the next three hours and just keep going'. I could see the white chalk of the cliffs of Dover from miles away, but in reality we were hours from landing.

"People ask me how I felt but I can't really remember feeling anything. I just thought I've got to keep swimming and that's that. Time does not really exist and before I knew it, I was within touching distance of the finish.

"You have got to walk three paces clear of the water before you are classed as having finished. I could feel rocks underneath my feet."

"Can I walk now?" she called to her boat. At last, her journey was almost over. Mr Mac encouraged her to take a few more strokes to avoid boulders and… then she was on her feet.

She clambered ashore, with only seagulls and seaweed-covered rocks to greet her. She scrambled over the rocks and fell into deep potholes. Standing upright on the beach, Brenda's swimsuit, heavily encrusted with salt, glistened.

Her landing at St Margaret's Bay was not made amid excited public scenes. This was because her victory had been largely unnoticed, unlike the progress of the overall winner. The only sign of her ordeal was a slight breathlessness and red-rimmed eyes from the salt of the Channel.

She raised one arm into the air, signalling she was all right, and then breathed a sigh of relief.

"Will someone tell my dad?"

6

In 1936, a nine-year-old Grimsby girl was paralysed down her left side after an attack of sunstroke. Now that same girl was Grimsby's Channel race record-breaker. She was the first woman ashore and had become the fastest woman to complete it.

Surrounded by flowers and with the bed covered in congratulatory messages, Brenda was made warm and cosy at her hotel, the Aintree, in Folkestone. There she was bathed by the hotel proprietress and got to bed at once – but not before the Press had taken a few photographs for prosperity.
It was midnight until she could finally settle down.

At the beach, she'd had no idea that she'd broken a record. She ate a piece of chocolate while undergoing the intense grease removal operation.

Brenda recovering after the swim

Undoubtedly one of the more unpleasant parts for a Channel swimmer of the 1950s, paraffin was applied liberally to her body with cotton to loosen the lanolin. That was rubbed off and her body then dried with more cotton. It was not long before she was in the launch boat, warmly swathed in cotton wool, dressed in a track suit and a bathing wrap, and on her way to Dover Harbour.

There, an enthusiastic crowd had gathered, having heard of her win. She left the beach, cheers ringing in her ears, holding lightly onto Jessie and Mr Mac. "I feel as though I could swim back," she told her mother over the telephone.

* * *

The following morning, Brenda woke up in her flower-filled bedroom at the Aintree Hotel, having swum the English Channel.

She had won the £1,000 prize offered by the Daily Mail to the first woman ashore. She was also the proud owner of the Festival of Britain cup for being the fastest woman and the Eva Peron trophy for being the first British woman to finish. And she felt just fine. That was, until she got out of bed.

"One of my first thoughts was to answer all of the messages of congratulations I had received," she recalls. "As my bare feet touched the floor, I winced. My feet were sore – very sore – because I had cut them on the rocks as I made it ashore below the cliffs, just south of St Margaret's Bay. I had cut them so badly that I had to limp around in bandages and soft shoes."

Brenda after the swim

But that didn't quell the feeling of immense happiness. She had a large breakfast of fried bread, toast and marmalade. At 9.30am, she had an appointment with journalist Maud Winterbourne. Her appearance in the lounge of the hotel caused considerable excitement. She was immediately surrounded by staff and well-wishers.

"I am not tired, and feel I could do it again," she told them. "But I think we will leave it for another year."

"Brenda told me she was the happiest girl in town," reported

Maud. "She was full of beans, happy and ready to chat with the scores of people lining up to congratulate her on her magnificent achievement."

Brenda told her: "I really am proud, proud and happy to have done so well in the race. The landing, I must confess, was awful. The coast was rock-strewn and I had the greatest difficultly in keeping my feet.

"I was determined I would walk out on my own two feet, and not crawl. As I stumbled and fell – I did not realise then how badly my feet were being cut – I was hoping that people watching me from the cliff top would not think I was unable to stand. I did want to land well. I knew I had finished the swim in good style.

"Mr McNally has trained us always to finish as well as, if not better than, when we started, and I knew I had done that. I did not want to spoil everything by crawling ashore.

"The last part of the swim had not been easy. The water got very rough and the tide was ebbing strongly – the strongest so far this year, I have been told. I got back into the boat, and my sister and trainer had me de-greased and wrapped in cotton wool and a robe in five minutes. I was so pleased with myself that I just let them get on with it and they did a good job.

"It was due to their treatment that I feel so grand this morning. I am still a little confused about what happened when I actually landed at Dover. I was given a lovely bouquet, someone rushed me off to a hut and gave me a hot milk drink.

"I was photographed for the newspapers and newsreels. I had to speak into a microphone. I believe I said, 'Thank you for giving me such a wonderful reception' but I am not quite sure.

"I was whisked off to the hotel where my landlady, Mrs G Reynaud, was waiting with a delightful hot bath. She shut us in the bathroom and scrubbed me all over. It was lovely. I felt horrible until I had had that bath, for I reeked of paraffin that had been used to clean off the grease. Then I went to bed and slept well."

Concluding the interview, she told Maud she was "ready for a good lunch".

A photo of some of the 1951 Channel swimmers

"This afternoon I am off to get my hair done. After that I sign 150 menus for the official reception and dinner tonight at Folkestone's Grand Hotel. For the dinner, I am wearing the only 'pretty' frock I have with me. It is of flowered purple silk."

She was a guest of honour at the Daily Mail's gala dinner, staged in the ballroom of the Grand. The fancy menu consisted of Crème Souveraine, Caneton d'Aylesbury Roti and Desires des Dames among other dishes.

"I didn't really know what I was eating," she later said, modestly, then going on to translate the dishes in precise detail.

By 10.30am, Brenda had received more than 40 telegrams of congratulations, including from the Mayor and Mayoress of Grimsby, which read: 'Grimsby is very proud of you. A warm welcome awaits you on your return'. There was also one from boyfriend Pat, which read: 'I knew you would do it'.

And there were three from Grimsby trawlers in Icelandic waters – her father's, the Leeds United, the Yardley and the Hertfordshire. Florence Chadwick, who successfully swam the Channel in 1950 and was planning to attempt a crossing on August 24, also sent a telegram.

Brenda told the media: "It is a relief to have it all over, but I would not have missed it for the world. It was a wonderful experience and well worth all the weeks of training and the anxiety waiting for the race to start. It is really good to feel you have justified people's faith in you. I know my trainer is delighted, and I know my mother and father are happy about it all."

Jessie, by Brenda's side, added: "We all knew she could do it. Brenda is going to swim the Channel again, with me next year. It is my one ambition to swim the Channel."

Reflecting on a momentous day, Mr Mac said: "You can make allowances for my enthusiasm if you like, but Brenda's swim was really a great performance. She was never in trouble and when she met those Goodwin currents a few miles off Dover we were a little worried. But Brenda fought on, only making little progress for a while, but gradually got used to the idea and surmounted this biggest obstacle with the greatest of ease."

The race was life-changing in a different way for competitor Eileen Fenton, from Dewsbury. She was dragged from the water suffering from loss of memory and mental exhaustion after swimming non-stop for nearly 13 hours. Afterwards, she decided to retire from long-distance swimming.

"That was my last Channel swim," she told the Yorkshire Post and Leeds Mercury's special correspondent in Folkestone. "I went straight to bed after I had been brought back here but I could not sleep. However, I do not feel too bad. I remember nothing of the last few hours I spent in the water. I had a black-out.

"I do not intend to take the risk of this happening again. So I shall give up long-distance swimming. Naturally I will not stop swimming altogether – I would be unhappy if I did. But from now on it will be short distances only."

The year before, she had won £1,000 for being the first woman home, from which expenses for both the 1950 and 1951 races were paid. But there was little money left, and Eileen had left her post as a teacher to concentrate on training, so was looking for a new appointment.

Brenda's prize cheque

Her situation shows how much swimming means to the swimmers. Despite having to pull out, the public supported her, and she was besieged by autograph hunters at her hotel – a fame that Grimsby's Brenda was also trying to get used to.

* * *

"One of those tiny specks of humanity battling against such a terrific mass of very unfriendly Channel." Brenda had done it. She breathed a deep sigh of relief, knowing Grimsby's unerring faith in her had been justified. And now she was getting ready to go home.

The first of the women competitors in the mass Channel swim to land on the English coast was naturally looking forward to leaving Folkestone for home turf.

The official figures for the swim were announced, confirming Brenda's time of 12 hours and 42 minutes. This beat the current women's record, held by US citizen Florence Chadwick, by 37 minutes. Overall, Brenda tied in fourth place with Egyptian Said el Arabi.

As fit as ever, she did not look like someone who had completed a challenge of heroic proportions. The Yorkshire Post commented that she "looked as if she might have stepped from behind a dress counter".

Brenda was rested, calm and collected, and more than prepared for a civic reception in her home town. Grimsby was waiting to applaud her feat.

"Cocktails, a civic dinner and a ceremonial drive through the town await her," wrote the Yorkshire Post and Leeds Mercury, under the headline 'Grimsby plans big welcome for girl Channel swimmer'. "And next month, when all the civic leaders have returned from holiday, there will be a full-scale Mayoral dinner in her honour."

She was in excellent spirits, telling the newspaper's correspondent that she intended to enter next year's race. Indeed, she felt happy enough to reveal a little about her background and motivation.

"I hope my 28-year-old sister, Jessie, will be able to swim with me," she said. "Jessie began long-distance swimming some time before I did. She used to swim with my brother. He was an RAF pilot and when he was shot down and killed during the war I started long-distance swimming to keep Jessie company. Jessie hoped to compete this year, but appendicitis stopped her training."

The journalist, from his base in Folkestone, wrote: "Hundreds of congratulatory messages have poured into Miss Fisher's hotel here as well as into her home at Grimsby. I am told that the telephone at her home has been ringing incessantly all day and that telegram boys were arriving every 20 minutes."

But Brenda wasn't going home to rest on her laurels. She was to resume her secretarial post to Councillor Arthur Drewry, head of a Grimsby fish curing company and president of the Football League, on the Monday, and was eager to get back into ballroom dancing. She had been forced to neglect her favourite pastime during training for the Channel, and was keen to get going again.

Meanwhile, her £1,000 prize money was to be deposited straight in the bank. "I shall have to pay next year's Channel swim expenses out of it," she told the reporter, thinking ahead as always.

In another interview, she said: "In many ways I shall not be sorry to get back to the normal round. This has been a truly wonderful time in my life."

The rounds of interviews and photographs continued. While she hit the headlines across the world, the Grimsby Evening Telegraph was reflecting on the special relationship it had with the champion. It had been almost alone among provincial newspapers in its coverage.

Radio listeners had been left mystified by the absence of news of Brenda during the race. The truth of the matter was that she and her group, led by Frenchman Morvan, were 'lost' in the Channel by the BBC commentators, the majority of newspaper correspondents and also by the control yacht Ginasal.

"Nowhere did this lack of attention to Brenda's progress appear more puzzling than in the editorial department of the Evening Telegraph," an article claimed. "Arrangements were made some weeks ago for special news coverage of the race and for speedy transmission of photographs.

"While accidents both afloat and ashore prevented all the pictures reaching Grimsby in time for publication, the stream of news bulletins never faltered in their flow or accuracy. Messages direct from Brenda's boat were transmitted to Dover and from there to the London office of the Evening Telegraph, whence they were relayed to Grimsby.

"These dispatches were in addition to the normal teleprinter service received over our private lines from the Press Association, the principal source of home news." In the early afternoon, Brenda's name disappeared from the reports on which most of the evening newspapers throughout the country were relying. Her group of swimmers failed to get a mention. The column headed by the Egyptians stole the news and they appeared to be the only contestants left in the race worthy of serious attention.

"In spite of the continued insistence by the BBC on the apparent supremacy of the Egyptian group, and contrary to the whole trend of the agency bulletins, the Evening Telegraph decided to accept as authoritative reports from its own observer, all of which reflected optimism and confidence in the ability of Brenda to outdistance her women rivals and even to challenge the men.

"Not until later was it disclosed that the BBC and the control yacht Ginasal had completely lost touch with the Morvan group.

"Only once, during the late afternoon, were Brenda's immediate followers assailed by doubt. It revealed itself in a message which reached the Evening Telegraph shortly before 5pm and stated that the Grimsby girl was being swept eastward by the current near the Goodwin Sands and was in danger of losing her lead. Even then, however, they were quick to point out that the set of the tide might well bring the Morvan swimmers back into the running, and such proved to be the case.

"Not only reporters but photographers concentrated their attention on the Egyptian group. The result was that Brenda's name leapt into the news, pictures of her battling her way to the English coast were almost unobtainable.

"Only Dennis Arnold, the Evening Telegraph chief photographer, had kept close to her party, and only he was in a position to satisfy the newspaper clamour for pictures of the Grimsby girl." Now, a race of a different kind began.

"His plates had been rushed by speedboat to Dover for transmission by wire to Hull and thence to Grimsby. Grievous misfortune overtook them, however.

"The messenger, misreading his instructions, sent them to London, and despatch to Grimsby was so long delayed that the Evening Telegraph was forced to go to press without them.

"In the circumstances, they were made available to the London Evening News, which carried in its main edition a large three-column wide picture taken by Dennis Arnold, the Evening Telegraph man-on-the-spot, and intended for his own paper."

7

Grimsby was proud and it would not be long until Brenda, close to tears, would see so for herself. The news of her success had gone everywhere. It was flashed onto the screen at cinemas throughout Grimsby and Cleethorpes, and those who didn't have time to create a reel simply announced it to the audiences, who greeted the news with wild cheering and rapturous applause.

A unique viewpoint of the race came in the form of a letter from S G Bingley to the Grimsby Evening Telegraph. He wrote: "Among many hundreds of passengers on board the Royal Daffodil, I should imagine my wife and I were surely the only Grimbarians.

Brenda at the cinema

"When approaching mid-Channel we came upon the first of the swimmers, and at reduced speed, came to at very close quarters. As each contestant was passed, the captain called for three encouraging cheers, which were readily forthcoming and in most cases were acknowledged by a wave of the hand from the swimmer. Some, however, took no heed of our cheering, and just continued the struggle.

"Eventually the captain announced the next competitor as 'The Girl From Grimsby' and again came the encouraging cheers. But this time we got a surprise, for the acknowledgement was nothing less than a vigorous wave with both hands at the same time, which brought spontaneous praise from all around, plus more cheers and a burst from the ship's siren."

Mr Bingley, a cinema manager, wrote: "At that moment I felt very proud of my home town, and more so, in fact, as so many strangers were feeling that way too. Reading this from the comfort of an armchair, the incident may appear to be relatively small, but when it is actually seen that one of those tiny specks of humanity battling against such a terrific mass of very unfriendly Channel makes such a splendid gesture, the sportsmanship therein is most worthy of recording.

"And as we passed the last of these heroes and I looked towards the white cliffs which would be the end of it all, it was a satisfying and stimulating thought that win or lose, the biggest ovation rightly went to 'The Girl From Grimsby.'"

'See the Conquering Heroine Comes!' declared a headline back home, while Brenda made preparations to return from Folkestone. It was front page news yet again for the Grimsby Evening Telegraph, triumphantly outlining the details of her homecoming reception.

Proud supporters waving their flags in Grimsby for Brenda's homecoming

The civic reception

"Many thousands of Lincolnshire men, women and children are planning the biggest welcome ever given to a girl from the county when their heroine, Brenda Fisher, returns to her home in Grimsby, the modest breaker of a cross-Channel swim record.

"Large crowds of well-wishers are expected to line parts of the route as her train passes through Lincolnshire. Brenda, who wins the Daily Mail prize of £1,000 and two cups for being the first woman home, is expected to leave Kings Cross at 4pm, arriving in Grimsby soon after 7.30pm. She had arranged to travel on the 1.18pm train but her family have made reservations on a later train.

"There will be a civic welcome waiting for her. The Deputy Mayor and Mayoress will be there to greet her on Grimsby Town Station, and the Mayor and Mayoress of Louth will be on Louth Station to add their personal tribute to her magnificent achievement.

"Brenda's route to the Town Hall will be: Town Station, Victoria Street, Cleethorpe Road, Riby Square, Freeman Street, Hainton Avenue, Wintringham Road, Doughty Road, Town Hall. People on the route are asked to display flags and bunting.

"The thousands of people expected to gather in Town Hall Square will hear the speech of welcome by Alderman Windley, which will be made on the Town Hall balcony. Another rather more formal civic welcome is under consideration for a later date."

For Brenda's mother, an anxious wait began. "I have not settled down to it at all," she told reporters. "I am so proud of her. She is a very, very clever girl."

Mrs Fisher spent the day visiting neighbours and making a vital trip into the town centre. "We have no plans and we shall go on just as usual," she said. "Brenda does not like any fuss. After we have had a family talk when father comes home from sea, I should say that Brenda will take the car to Cleethorpes and sit on the prom or go to Skegness for the day.

"Of course there is the civic reception – which she is dreading. When we have settled down Brenda may express a desire to do something in particular."

* * *

The homecoming reception, to Brenda, was a greater ordeal than the race. Grimsby's own Queen of the Channel received a royal welcome, which began on the train as she travelled back to Lincolnshire. People began to gather at stations and level crossings as far south of the county as Boston, and as Brenda's train came north, crowds numbered in their hundreds. At Louth, there was a three-minute stop, with people lining the platform. Brenda was heard to utter: "Oh, I appreciate this very much" and an onlooker said: "It brought a lump to my throat."

At Grimsby, a staggering sixty thousand well-wishers turned out; the largest crowd at that point to have ever gathered in the town. The train station was bedecked with flags and draped with bunting, and a red carpet was laid at the entrance.

Porters wore button-holes and welcoming smiles, and passengers alighting from earlier trains had waited for the next train carrying Grimsby's important cargo. A stark contrast to the dark, deep and silent depths of the Channel, Brenda's homecoming was bright, loud and overwhelming.

It was a breathless Brenda who, near to tears, later told the twenty thousand people who had made it to Town Hall Square: "I think I would rather swim the Channel."

Congratulatory messages

So just what was it like to see throngs

Crowds of people in Town Hall Square

of people, numbering in their thousands? "It was a shock!" she says. "I remember being on the train and thinking, 'What on earth is going on, surely these people aren't here for me?' I thought there must have been something else happening."

As the train arrived into Grimsby, the reception committee readied itself with bouquets and congratulations.

"A tanned face and a mass of platinum blonde hair were framed in the carriage window," reported the Grimsby Evening Telegraph. Their owner stepped down and embraced a woman who walked nervously forward. 'Oh mum,' said Brenda, 'It's good to be back.'"

Photographers from scores of national newspapers and agencies, patiently waiting, spent several minutes with the sporting champion. The shutters clicked as she was greeted by the Deputy Mayor, and flash bulbs popped as she was joyously reunited with relatives and friends. Officials, the reception committee and police officers offered their warm wishes, all the while under the gaze of cameramen's lenses.

Nervously biting her lip, she stood on the red carpet, feet close together, holding onto a huge bouquet. A nice touch was the presence of Cleethorpes dentist Hadyn Taylor, who had conquered the Channel before the war.

"The party moved off," the Telegraph's reporter observed. "The cheers – the first of near two hours of cheers – began. And there was a special cheer for 'Good old Herbert', as trainer McNally followed the main party at a distance."

The following hours are a bewildering memory to the modest, somewhat shy Brenda, who at this moment in time was the greatest British-born female long-distance swimmer in the world.

There were people, people everywhere… crowds were six feet deep and beyond. There was no room to move on Station Approach. Victoria Street, Riby Square, Hainton Avenue… Grimsby's main thoroughfares were jammed tight with masses of good-humoured well-wishers.

Bunting was hanging from every possible place and flags were flying from poles, windows and doorways. Buses were desperately trying to pick a way through the masses with little luck. In fact, on realising they were failing fast, many drivers, conductors and passengers simply gave up and joined in the ovation. It was a scene of magnitude and unlike anything the town had seen before.

Margaret and Ron Limb, who have lived in Grimsby all of their lives, were a young married couple living in Pasture Street when they braved the crowds to see Brenda.

Margaret says: "We decided we wanted to see her at the Town Hall. I had never seen anything like that since the war ended, and I never have since either, it was that exciting. It was big news for Grimsby and it felt as if the entire world had turned out. She had done us a huge service and made us proud."

Ron adds: "It was a wonderful thing, and still is. Nowadays swims across the Channel seem so hi-tech. It was an amazing feat.

"It did not take us long to walk from Pasture Street, but the crowds lined every single pavement, and were three or four people deep. We did struggle to get through and eventually just had to follow the crowd. We got there, and people were chattering and waiting for Brenda to appear. When the door opened on the balcony of the Town Hall, there was an intake of breath and then cheering like you've never heard… there was just a great big roar, and it was deafening!

"She gave a shy wave and we went mad. Looking at her, you wouldn't think she had done such a magnificent thing; she was so unassuming. It was as if the entire world was there, cheering and shouting. I seemed to stop breathing, it was so exciting.

"It certainly was a big event for Grimsby."

*   *   *

The small convoy made its way slowly around the town centre. Brenda was on the roof of the Mayoral car, holding tightly onto the Daily Mail Festival Cup with one arm and waving with the other. Mr Mac was by her side, quite rightly acknowledging his share of the plaudits. Other cars followed, containing family, friends and officials, supported by the police.

It was growing dark by the time the convoy reached its destination, Grimsby Town Hall. In the square beyond, police officers linked arms and formed human barriers to hold back the crowds while Brenda stepped down and out of the car. She waved and disappeared into the foyer. The patient crowd waited for some minutes, and then the rousing chant of 'We want Brenda!' and 'Queen of the Channel!' began.

"The thousands in the rear pressed forward on the thousands at the front," wrote the Grimsby Evening Telegraph. "For the thin blue line of police, it was an unequal battle.

More wellwishers

"The line retreated, in good order, and the crowd, overspilling from every foot of the square, and from the adjacent streets, surged to within yards of the Town Hall doors.

"'We want Brenda,' from the people in the square. 'We want Brenda,' from the small boys perched on top of a bus shelter. 'We want Brenda' from the scores on a roof top opposite.

"Through the entrance to a balcony floodlit and decked with flowers, stepped a trim, neat figure in a brown costume, cameo brooch on the lapel. The chant changed to cheers."

This electrifying atmosphere thrilled and worried Brenda with equal force. The cameo brooch, mentioned in the newspaper report, had been presented by Pat just moments before, and she remembers how he secured it to her lapel with affection and pride shining in his eyes. Little touches from the people who meant most to her got the shy girl through the ordeal.

"There was no such thing as media training or anything like that," she recalls. "We'd talked about the reaction, obviously, but I honestly had no idea the outpouring was going to be quite like that. It was unbelievable. I had never seen so many people in my life, and have never done since.

"It was a night of mixed emotions. I went from feeling almost deliriously happy one moment to being terrified the next. As you might have gathered, I did not take to all the public and 'fame' side of things very well. I understood that the attention was because the public was proud of my achievement, but all I really wanted to do was go home.

"I would hate that to come across as ungrateful or dismissive, because I really am not. I have never felt such a rollercoaster of emotions, and it was so overwhelming I wanted to hide! Yet, at exactly the same time, I wanted to hug each and every person who had braved the crush to see me. That reaction meant so much to me at that moment that I can't really put it into words.

"I remember seeking out my mother's face as

Crowds in the streets

the train drew in at the station and feeling such relief sweep over me. Having my family there kept me anchored, and less nervous – only a little less, mind! I was just a 23-year-old lass from Lincolnshire and all of a sudden, the world's focus was on me. It would be enough to throw anyone!"

The Deputy Mayor, Alderman W H Windley, was the first to make an official speech. "Your brilliant success in swimming the Channel at your first attempt and in a shorter time than any other woman reflects the greatest credit upon you for your courage and endurance in what must surely be one of the most gruelling and exhausting athletic contests in the world," he told Brenda.

"We are all very proud that it is the seaport of Grimsby that so appropriately produced the competitor with the pluck, skill and stamina necessary to lead the way across the English Channel in the front of others selected from swimmers all over the world.

"You have received a right royal welcome and we deeply regret that we are not celebrating a double victory tonight. Had it not been for her unfortunate illness, sister Jessie may have been with you."

Indeed, Jessie was anything but forgotten in the celebrations. She was treated to a special cheer by the crowd of thousands, which she acknowledged with a shy wave of the hand. Mr Mac thanked all contributors to the Brenda Fisher Fund and the vice-chairman of the fund committee, Mr G T Baker, echoed his remarks.

"This was more nerve-wracking than swimming the Channel," laughed Brenda, when asked by journalists for her thoughts. "I am proud to have won for Grimsby. Thank you all – very much."

* * *

Windyridge, Brenda's home in a quiet area of Grimsby, was floodlit upon her return. She was delighted by the response, but also amused; again struggling with those swinging emotions.

"I was so happy that I had made Grimsby proud," she continues, trying to articulate just exactly what she was feeling. "I've already admitted that I found it a little awkward to be the centre of attention. I am just not that type of character, so it was rather funny. I was just someone who had completed a swim, albeit an important one. Others have done much greater things, but the warmth I felt from my home town was enormous. That made me happiest of all – that I had done everyone proud."

In truth, she was exhausted ("more exhausted than swimming for hours") and it was the sight of twenty thousand people gazing up at her as she stepped onto the balcony at Grimsby Town Hall which had shocked her to the core.

"It was strange," she explains, holding her swimmer's hands tightly in her lap. "That moment was unreal. It was like I was watching a film. It did not really sink in until I got home and had time to reflect on what had just happened. At one point, I started chuckling and could not stop for a while. It was all so bizarre!"

The day after the homecoming, she told a reporter: "I am almost afraid to go out. People everywhere crowd round me and stop to offer their congratulations. I just want to forget the excitement and settle down to a quiet life and my work.

"I shall not be doing any more serious swims this year. On Tuesday I shall take my 'adopted' niece, Susanne Macklam, to the Cleethorpes Baths, teaching her to swim. Then on Saturday I hope to give a demonstration at Cleethorpes on the way I swam the Channel so people who raised £300 to pay for my training can see me in action."

That afternoon she filled her car with flowers and drove to Springfield Hospital, where she gave them to women patients in block four who had sent her a telegram. Then she visited housebound 75-year-old Anna Mills, in Freshney Street, who composed a poem for Brenda.

That night, Pat, her mother and sister drove to see some friends in Cleethorpes and to see if Brenda was mentioned on the TV weekly newsreel flashback. They were disappointed when it only showed footage of the men's finish.

However, Grimsby's champion was looking forward and was soon back at work. Her office, in Maclure Street on the docks, was decorated with flags and bunting in her honour. Employer Arthur Drewry said: "I told her she could have two or three days away from work but she asked to come back."

Sombre warehouses were trimmed with flags and chalked slogans, including 'Good old Brenda' and 'Channel Avenue'. As she entered the office, people slapped her on the shoulder and she was presented with some home-grown flowers.

At Windyridge, it seemed as if there was always someone at the door. Among the many visitors were four little girls, who knocked timidly. They carried a circular piece of cardboard on which they had written 'Welcome home, Brenda!' and a drawing of three swimmers. For a while, the card hung on the front gate of Windyridge, an acknowledgement of Brenda's achievement and she, in turn, thanking everyone for their support.

Brenda back at work in the office

Journalist Peter Chapman, who wrote under the name Odd Man Out in the Grimsby Evening Telegraph, was just the scribe to succinctly put into words why Brenda had made waves.

"Amid all the well-deserved tributes to Miss Fisher for her tremendous feat of endurance and pluck, what I think stands out above all is her modesty," he penned. "In these days, when so many people, and more especially the younger generation, adopt the attitude that if they do not blow their own trumpet, nobody will blow it for them, it is a change to find a girl who does not allow a weight of praise, however well deserved, to turn her head.

"With it all, she retains that calm, almost aloof outlook which has always been one of her chief characteristics during her many successes in swimming and other spheres. By the way, when Mr Haydn Taylor swam the Channel on August 22, 1935, he covered the distance in 14 hours 48 minutes.

"Of course Miss Fisher had the spur of competing against others for a big prize, but nevertheless the respective times do show what a remarkable feat it was by this young lady.

"One of the marvels of the Channel swim was, of course, the organisation of news transmission from numerous craft of all size criss-crossing from one swimmer to another. Reports were collected and centralised at a control centre afloat and sent through to a Marconi marine radio unit to a GPO link ashore. Some of the photographs taken by Evening Telegraph chief photographer Dennis Arnold were developed on the parent ship, and then direct to Dover, sent by radio to London and thence to their final destination. It was all a wonderful demonstration of modern methods in radio and newspaper circles."

Pat is pictured here pinning a brooch to Brenda's lapel at Grimsby Town Hall

Brenda being praised on her victory

8

Brenda's star had risen, and her fame stretched way beyond Lincolnshire. She was an international celebrity.

The South African cricket team sent Brenda a bunch of beautiful flowers to mark her success. Since then, she has always called them her "good

Brenda being presented with a bouquet from the cricket team

omen". From the Aberdeen Evening Express to the Dundee Courier, no corner of the media left Brenda's story uncovered.

However, it was at home where Brenda's heart was touched the most. Before she was halfway across the Channel, Grimsby Town Hall's steps were being measured for the red carpet, whatever the result. Grimsby Corporation, on behalf of the townspeople, honoured the "great and courageous girl" at a special ceremony. Members of the public cheered loudly from the gallery as she was presented with a medallion and an inscribed silver salver.

At a dinner that followed, the Mayor, in his toast, said: "It took a certain man with the whole German Army, Navy and Air Force behind him five years to do something which took Brenda Fisher 12 hours and 42 minutes to achieve. "Miss Fisher has not only brought renown to herself but a reflected glory on her native town."

Brenda replied: "My feelings on reaching the English shore are not easy to define but high among them was pride that I belonged to Grimsby, whose seafarers have always played a great part in both peace and war."

Next, the Fish Merchants' Association directors and staff presented her with a solid silver dressing table set.

She went to Louth to open a ball at the town hall on behalf of Louth Old Age Pensioners' Building Fund, and a crowd of sightseers pitched up on the steps outside. Laryngitis prevented her from making a speech but she was presented with a bouquet by swimsuit-clad seven-year-olds Diane Monument and Christine Rushby. She danced the first waltz with orchestra leader Wylie Price, and then signed autographs for a shilling to raise money for the fund.

When Brenda walked into the Reynolds' Royal School of Dancing, she met herself. She was greeted by a tailor's dummy wearing Brenda's own bathing wrap and goggles, carrying a towel. It was part of the decorations for her visit. There was also a double lifesize portrait of a photograph taken by the Grimsby News. Notices read 'Congratulations Channel Queen'.

Brenda was overwhelmed; 200 of her dancing friends had turned out to see her unveil the new honours board of 400 names, including her own. Three-year-old Peggy Jubb gave her a bouquet twice the child's size. Nine-year-old Julie Waterhouse, 12-year-old Wendy Foster and John Macullie offered gifts. John stood like a gentlemen while Brenda kissed him.

At Scunthorpe's Pavilion Cinema, more than two thousand schoolchildren watched a complete newsreel of the race. The film had been specially ordered by the cinema for the youngsters to watch for free, who had sent Brenda a pair of spare goggles.

In one evening alone, she and Jessie went to the Grimsby and District Schools' Sports Association Maddock Cup Swimming Gala (6.45pm), then she opened the Wellington Ward of the Conservative and Unionist Association's Christmas Fair and craft party (7.30pm) and then changed for a Conservative ball in North Somercotes.

She was a surprise guest at a Cub weekend, gave an address at Ashby Townswomen's Guild, attended the annual dinner of the Grimsby branch of the National Association of Cycle Traders, visited Goxhill and Healing Women's Institutes, the Flottergate Men's Association and the Grimsby Mouse Society's annual social. She was given the honorary office of vice president of the British Legion No 1 branch women's section, watched a News of the World regional darts final, visited the Crusaders Cricket Club, was guest at the Grimsby and North Lincolnshire Press Ball, and opened dozens of fetes.

Brenda being notoriously introvert, Jessie was mostly by her side. On Brenda's behalf, she gave about 30 slideshow presentations and 24 talks in just a few weeks. Brenda said: "I am very proud of my birthplace and honoured that I can call myself a Grimbarian and if, by being successful in my swimming, I have helped in any way to put Grimsby on the map, then I am proud to have been able to do so. I am very proud to belong to Grimsby and this will be an undying memory for me."

But there was one glaring omission from the joyous outpourings in very early days of her victory – her father.

* * *

It was not until August 20 that Brenda was reunited with her father for the first time since becoming a swimming heroine. In a radio message, Mr Fisher had told his daughter: "Most wonderful performance Brenda. What I expected from you, darling. All Grimsby ships at White Sea greatly interested. God bless you, love Dad."

His youngest child was waiting for him on a boat as Skipper Albert Fisher entered the River Humber in the last stage of his voyage home to Grimsby

Brenda with her father on his boat

from a White Sea fishing trip. She closed her eyes through fear of falling into the water as she clambered onto the Leeds United and into her father's arms. It was the first time she had been aboard her father's boat at sea since she was a child.

Mr Fisher said: "Bless you sweetheart, you clever girl. How are you Blondie? It has not hurt you?"

Brenda replied: "I'm fine Daddy. Are you really proud of me?"

They celebrated with tea and chocolate biscuits. In his cabin below deck, they caught up. He had been 1,000 miles away when Brenda was in the water.

"I listened to the radio for news of Blondie and there was none. I could not eat and I smoked more than 50 cigarettes. I felt so very far from her. When I received a cable from the Daily Mail telling me she was the first woman ashore I went 'bubbly' inside," he told journalists.

"All 19 members of the crew who could be spared from watch were crowding round the radio on the bridge and I gave them three bottles of rum when I knew Brenda had been successful. Then I was home as fast as possible. I longed to be with Brenda while she was swimming but I am perhaps glad I was not there to see and hear everyone cheering, for in my pride at her achievement I might have made myself look foolish."

A member of the crew told reporters how Mr Fisher kept walking out on the moonlit deck, saying

Brenda with her father's crew

"Blondie's done it". Mr Fisher added: "My chest has expanded two feet since the swim."

Onlookers were noisier in their joy, and the river was filled with the sound of hooting ship's sirens. Holidaymakers and day trippers crowded the sides of the paddleship Tattershall Castle as it passed near Skipper Fisher's trawler, shouting and cheering enthusiastically.

"As Brenda clambered over the trawler's rail, her first action was to turn towards the stern where the bulk of the ship's crew were standing. 'Thank you for your telegram', she said." The Grimsby Evening Telegraph was, as ever, on hand to report the proceedings. All of these newspaper articles are today carefully treasured by Brenda.

"During the family greetings, the crew of the trawler were busy getting out all the flags in the signal locker and 'dressing ship' in her honour," the report continued.

Brenda had travelled out into the Humber from the Grimsby Dock basin in the section tug Invigilator to await her father's arrival on the Leeds United. She was accompanied by Jessie and Pat, swimmer Eric Macklam and his young daughter Susanne. Councillor J Mawer, outside manager of Consolidated Fisheries, which owned the Leeds United, joined the party with his wife and Mr J V Chatburn, secretary of the Grimsby Steam Fishing Vessels Mutual Insurance and Protecting Co Ltd.

The Telegraph's report takes up the story: "As the tug left the basin, a smudge of smoke on the horizon showed that a trawler was approaching Spurn Point. But the question was which trawler? The Leeds United and the York City were both due in on the same tide, and the ships are identical sister ships.

"When Mr Mawer, who studied the vessel closely through a pair of binoculars, announced 'It is the Leeds United', Skipper Frederick Grant, of the Invigilator, blew a double cock-crow on his ship's siren. The deep bass of Leeds United's siren bellowed a reply, and a moment later Skipper Fisher emerged from the wheelhouse and waved an answer to Brenda, who was waving furiously, her blonde hair ruffled by the wind.

"A few minutes later, Leeds United's anchor went down, the tug swung in a circle, drew alongside and was made fast. The Tattershall Castle again passed, and passengers crowded to the rail as the ship's siren gave her its welcome.

"From the trawler's bridge, Brenda waved her thanks and then dived into the wheelhouse where she blew a cock-crow on the siren. Other ships passing by altered course to pass close to the Leeds United and add their whistled congratulations."

These scenes of jubilation warmed Brenda's heart.

When the pair had reunited, Skipper Fisher had more time to express his thoughts to the Press. "I am naturally very proud indeed of her, but it is only what I expected," he said. "I knew she was a strong swimmer and, for a distance swimmer, a fast swimmer, and I felt all the time that she would get across so long as nothing unfortunate happened. My only regret is that Jessie was not there with her, for I feel sure that she would have got across as well."

He had a word of criticism for the lack of radio coverage of the race. "I heard all the wireless broadcast commentaries upon the race, but the less I say about that, the better. At times it seemed as if there were only Egyptians and a Frenchman swimming."

But he added: "I have hardly eaten anything since Thursday. I was too excited to want any food."

From then on, the GY386 Leeds United remained in Brenda's heart, a painting of which hangs in the living room at Windyridge today.

* * *

It was an 'umbrella welcome' for Grimsby's champion swimmer when she drove to Cleethorpes for a civic reception on Thursday, August 30, 1951. The Grimsby Evening Telegraph was there to report on the scene.

"Even the rain failed to dampen the warmth of the welcome at the Park Street boundary," it wrote, "where a wet but enthusiastic crowd collected to see the Mayor and Mayoress, Councillor and Mrs C J Shaw, greet Brenda beneath a canopy of umbrellas."

"First stop in the subsequent tour of the town was the Council House," the report continued, "where Brenda, wearing an attractive pink two-piece suit of corded silk, met and was entertained to tea by the members of the corporation and their wives." The Mayor presented her with a silver casket on behalf of the town, exclaiming: 'A formal introduction is not necessary for Brenda.'

"Although she is not a Cleethorpes girl we have a proprietary interest in her, for she has spent many happy hours in our town. Congratulations on a wonderful achievement and congratulations, too, to trainer Mr H McNally, who deserves as much praise as Brenda," he said.

Brenda, reluctant in her fame, replied: "I suppose I should be used to this by now but I am afraid I am not, so I will just say thank you very much." Then, the triumphant tour of the town began, in the company of her parents, sister Jessie and her husband, Mr Mac and Pat.

It started with a visit to the bathing pool, where Brenda had spent many hours with Jessie. The Grimsby and District Swimming Association gala was being played out to a crowd, who gave the champion a warm reception. The next port of call was the Ritz Cinema, in Grimsby Road, where a packed audience gave her three hearty cheers.

She was greeted by thirteen-year-old Brenda Costello, of Constitutional Avenue, Cleethorpes, who presented her with an alarm clock and lampshade. The gifts had been bought by members of the Ritz ABC Minors' Matinee Club, and the cinema manager, William Connolly, gave her a copy of the Pathe newsreel showing her arrival on the south coast. "If you want to show it to your friends, bring it here and I will put it on," he told her.

Brenda's tour then went onto the Empire Theatre and the Pier Pavilion, where she was introduced by the chairman of the Pier Committee, Councillor J Magee. Stop-offs at the Café Dansant and the Winter Gardens – well known Cleethorpes entertainment venues – followed.

In the weeks and months following the race, Brenda remained a much-loved and admired figure in Grimsby, and indeed the wider region.

Production temporarily slowed down at the town's famous Tickler's jam factory when she donned a white coat and, with sister Jessie and Pat by her side, tried her hand at an automatic jam-filling machine. The management were delighted to receive a visit from the high-profile sportswoman. On the day of the swim, the factory radio was constantly tuned in to inform anxious workers of Brenda's progress.

Learning that she had been invited to tour the factory, they held a collection and bought her some lovely pink flowers, even though the factory had already contributed to the Brenda Fisher Fund.

The event was captured for prosperity in a quaintly written Grimsby Evening

Brenda trying Tickler's jam

Telegraph report: "Overall pockets had hidden autograph books throughout the morning, but as Brenda arrived, fruit-stained hands gripped the books, open at a blank page, and with a word of congratulation the girls stepped forward to ask for her autograph. Although for a time Brenda 'stopped a lot of jam-jars from leaving the factory', the girls made up for the lost time, as she satisfied each autograph-hunter with her signature and a modest smile."

Obviously Brenda could not leave without trying some of that famous Tickler's jam, and upon visiting the canteen, there was a special surprise waiting for her. Miss Maude Flint, who had worked at the factory for 35 years and was the canteen manageress, had baked an iced cake for Brenda to take home.

GYT 977 GTG 9.47 PM

GRIMSBY T 20 =

GREETINGS BRENDA FISHER

WINDYRIDGE SCARTHOE RD

GRIMSBY =

SINCERE CONGRATULATIONS UPON YOUR

BRILLIANT FEAT =

FELLOW PASSENGERS NUMBER 9 BUS 11.0 PM +

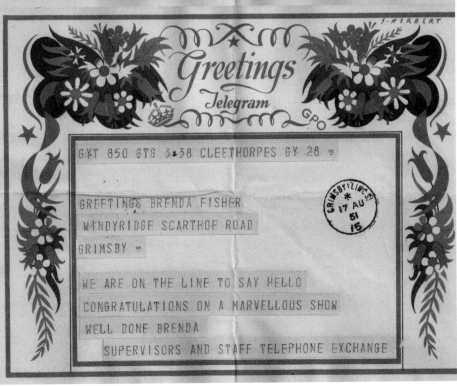

GYT 850 GTG 3.38 CLEETHORPES GY 28 =

GREETINGS BRENDA FISHER

WINDYRIDGE SCARTHOE ROAD

GRIMSBY =

WE ARE ON THE LINE TO SAY HELLO

CONGRATULATIONS ON A MARVELLOUS SHOW

WELL DONE BRENDA

SUPERVISORS AND STAFF TELEPHONE EXCHANGE

85

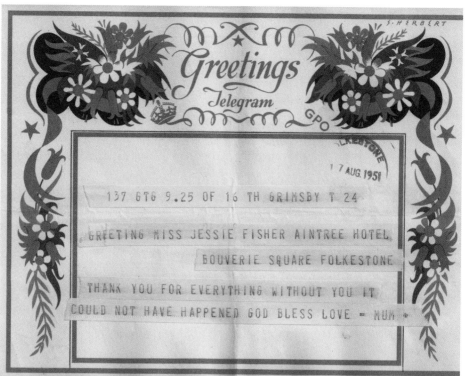

Greetings Telegram GPO

S. HERBERT

FOLKESTONE
1 7 AUG. 1951

137 GTG 9.25 OF 16 TH GRIMSBY T 24

GREETING MISS JESSIE FISHER AINTREE HOTEL
BOUVERIE SQUARE FOLKESTONE

THANK YOU FOR EVERYTHING WITHOUT YOU IT
COULD NOT HAVE HAPPENED GOD BLESS LOVE = MUM +

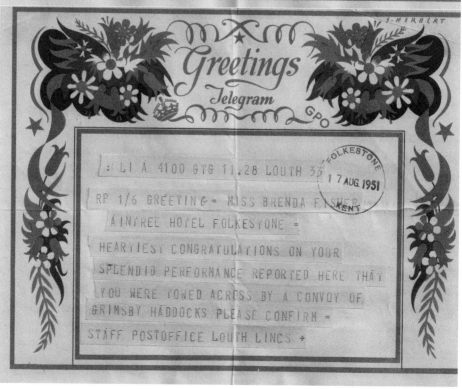

Greetings Telegram GPO

S. HERBERT

FOLKESTONE
1 7 AUG. 1951
KENT

: LI A 4100 GTG 11.28 LOUTH 35

RP 1/6 GREETING = MISS BRENDA FISHER
AINTREE HOTEL FOLKESTONE =
HEARTIEST CONGRATULATIONS ON YOUR
SPLENDID PERFORMANCE REPORTED HERE THAT
YOU WERE TOWED ACROSS BY A CONVOY OF
GRIMSBY HADDOCKS PLEASE CONFIRM =
STAFF POSTOFFICE LOUTH LINCS +

9

Radiant in a commemorative dressing gown she was given after swimming the Channel, Brenda walked onto the stage at the Victoria Palace, London. Here she was, a girl from Grimsby, centre stage at the 1951 Royal Command Performance… on the boards Elizabeth Taylor trod.

Stepping out into the spotlight of the famous theatre alongside other sporting greats of the time did not faze her one bit. "I just had to stand there while they said what we had done and be applauded," she says. "I was very much relieved!"

Brenda's mother framed a photograph of the cast, assembled on stage; Brenda is standing behind comedienne and actress Gracie Fields. Other stars on the bill included Harry Secombe, The Wiere Brothers, the Marie de Vere dancers, Richard Murdoch and Kenneth Horne, Arthur English, Alan and Blanche Lund, Pearl Primus and Patricia Morison.

Brenda recalls how Michael Standing, the Head of Variety at the BBC, had some stern words for the audience being recorded. Everyone was issued with a 'dos and don'ts' leaflet, which read: "We are very glad to welcome you to this broadcast. You are important to the show and add to the pleasure of listeners at home. You can also, quite unintentionally, achieve exactly the opposite results by showing a little too much enthusiasm and by clapping at unsuitable points.

"May I therefore ask you to bear in mind that we welcome your laughter at any time, and we hope for your applause, but in appropriate places only, that is, at the end of a scene or musical number, or on the entrance or exit of an artist who you think deserves it. But we do not want clapping for individual gags or jokes during an act or scene. It holds up the programme and often spoils the show for listeners. We do not want catcalls, whistles and cheers. They make a horrible noise 'on the air'."

Brenda took part in an item called The Champ, theatreland's tribute to British sport, and the stars were presented to the audience by Bud Flanagan and Chesney Allen. Thrilled to make an appearance, she walked down the centre stage staircase.

A great round of applause came from the audience. Princess Margaret turned to her mother and made several remarks, while both clapped enthusiastically. Then Brenda moved to the side of the stage, where she joined Stanley Matthews.

The other stars involved in The Champ read like a Who's Who of the sporting world at the time: Reg Harris (cycling); Don Cockell (boxing); Geoff Duke (motorcycling); Reg Parnell (motor racing); Johnny Leach (table tennis); Geoffrey Paish and Dorothy Round (lawn tennis); Jack Young (speedway); Joe Davis (snooker); Gus Risman (rugby); Leslie Reynolds (greyhound racing); Stubby Mason and Duke Campbell (ice hockey); McDonald Bailey and Sidney Wooderson (running); Jeanette Altwegg (ice skating); E H Temme and Tom Blower (Channel swimmers); Freddie Brown (cricket); Gordon Richards (horseracing); and the Cambridge boat crew.

So what was it like sharing the limelight with northern, working class Gracie, the highest paid actress in Britain during the 1930s?

"It was a lovely experience," she says. "Gracie looked very glamorous indeed. The theatre was a very grand place. I didn't meet the Royals but I was very proud to have taken part, and I know my family were proud too. Doing things like the Command Performance just seemed to happen."

That year's audience was surprised when the Royal party arrived, for along with the Queen and Princess Margaret were nurses Ruth Beswetherick and Doreen Pearce, who had been nursing His Majesty King George VI through a recent illness.

His Majesty was too ill to attend the Victoria Palace but as Her Majesty the Queen told an enquiring Bud Flanagan: "He is going on very nicely, thank you." And when told how sorry everyone was that His Majesty could not attend, the Queen responded: "So is he, but he is listening in."

Life had changed dramatically for Grimsby's own queen, in ways she never imagined. First and foremost, Brenda had to accept – and become used to – the fact that she was a celebrity. Not only that, she was a star in demand and a bona fide celebrity of the day.

Standing shoulder to shoulder with fellow athletes, she was a sporting great and an ambassador of her generation. Her striking blonde hair and no-nonsense manner made her stand out from the crowd.

She wore beautifully tailored clothes and her boyfriend was a footballer. For young girls, she became an idol. For young people in general, she was proof that you could conquer anything if you tried hard enough.

In Grimsby, she was given the closest thing to a star on the Hollywood Walk of Fame. A tug was named Brenda Fisher in her honour, launched at Harker's Shipyard, in Knottingley, Yorkshire, in 1955. It tended the trawler fleets 24 hours a day for 25 years and also towed bigger vessels out of the fish docks.

Well-known jeweller Arthur Hewitt worked for 55 years in his family's business in Victoria Street, Grimsby, from the age of 15 until he was 70. He presented Brenda with a Rolex watch to acknowledge her Channel swim; at the time, Rolex watches were one of the only waterproof types. Skegness' Butlin's Holiday Park offered her placement as a swimming instructor for what was a handsome wage of £10 a week.

On a national scale, she was crowned Sportswoman of the Year 1951. She was a guest at the first ever Sports Writers' Association dinner to the sportswomen of Britain, held at the Criterion, in Piccadilly, London, on October 3. There, she told the assembled guests: "I am told I am the fastest British-born Channel swimmer. Was I tired? Never. My only fear was that I might have to crawl out of the water instead of walk out."

The Brenda Fisher tug

* * *

Jessie, meanwhile, was once again feeling the pull of the water. In 1952, a year after she had been foiled in her English Channel attempt by appendicitis, she was back in Morecambe Bay for the fourth time. She fought sea sickness and cramp – and the loss of the lens from her googles – to record her fastest time and gain second place in the women's record of just two hours and 43 minutes. She had only been in training for four months – after years out of swimming. The last time she'd been in the water for a contest was in Morecambe in 1947. The water was choppy and it was the first time Jessie experienced sea sickness. She'd had difficulty breathing, which meant she had swallowed water.

"I have achieved all I had hoped for, to complete the swim and to restore my self-confidence," she told reporters, grinning. "I am ashamed of myself. I was seasick during the race for the first time in my life!"

"Like me, swimming was at the core of Jessie," recalls Brenda, happily. "I was so proud of her; it really did do wonders for her confidence. The Channel incident had upset her greatly. It had been our big dream, and for it to be dashed like that was just awful."

For Brenda, time was passing quickly. 1952 came and went, and with 1953 came a new business venture. "The company challenges any woman in the world to compete with Brenda in a swim over a distance of 30 miles or more."

At 26 and now engaged to be married, Brenda - or rather her name - became an enterprise. Brenda Fisher Enterprise Ltd was formed in Blackpool to exploit her "name and reputation". The new company's nominal capital was £1,000 in £1 shares, and its objects, according to Jordan's Daily Register of new companies, was "to exploit for commercial purposes the name and reputation in all parts of the world". It would also "carry on the business, professions or trades of professional sportsmen, stage, film, radio and television actors and broadcasters".

The directors were Brenda and Morecambe businessman Mark Shaw, who became Brenda's manager. He was the inventor of the Marksway "unsinkable" swimsuit, at that point setting his sights on turning Brenda into an international star.

Mr Shaw was quoted in the Press as saying: "The new company will sponsor all of Brenda's attempts to establish her as the world's greatest long distance swimmer."

The challenge remained unmet – and all the while, Brenda was eyeing up another epic swim to take up most of 1954.

Brenda holding her trophy

10

In August 1954, Brenda became the second woman to swim the Channel twice. Overall, she came third in the race, that year sponsored by Butlin's, after almost 15 hours in the water. And although she admitted it was tougher than in 1951 and a very hard crossing, she was fit enough to go dancing that evening.

At first, few people had realised she had landed. There were no officials to meet her at St Margaret's Bay, and more than an hour had elapsed before they knew she had finished. By that time, she was already resting at her hotel in Folkestone.

Even though she had been through this once before, the thrill of the race was not lost on anyone. Today, the pages of Press coverage still make exciting reading. The challenge began at 12.30am with Billy Butlin himself firing a Very light into the sky.

The three women and twelve men plunged into the sea at Cap Gris Nez. There should have been another entrant, Jenny James, from Pontypridd, but she withdrew at the last minute. She had made the journey to France with her trainer but was not fit enough to participate. Like Jessie, one can only imagine the heartbreak and frustration she was experiencing.

Within two and a half hours of the start, Britain had lost one of her strongest challengers, 28-year-old Kenneth Wray, from Southport. He had been going well but had to retire due to a strained shoulder. Kenneth returned immediately to Folkestone and told reporters that when the swimmers entered the water, they found the temperature slightly higher than expected – at almost 60 degrees.

He said: "I didn't see Brenda Fisher but I am told that at the start she was going strongly, swimming easily and making fast progress."

For the following few hours, nothing was heard from the swimmers as they ploughed through the darkness in the quiet, cold Channel. With the dawn came news of Brenda's progress.

At 9am she was three-quarters of the way across, behind male competitors Baptista Pereira and Marie Hassen Hammad, leaving just one question on the lips of the thousands of spectators waiting at Folkestone and Dover - "Can Brenda catch up and beat the men?"

* * *

Brenda at Butlins

The media once again went wild for Brenda, and nor was the excitement lost on Grimsby's residents. Oldroyd's shop, in the Old Market Place, had a chart of the Channel from Cap Gris Nez to Dover and gave up-to-date progress reports of the swim by moving markers every hour. In the days when extra editions were the norm, newspapers wound the anticipation up to fever pitch.

"Grimsby's Brenda Fisher was at 2.45pm this afternoon only about half-a-mile from the shore in the international cross-Channel race," wrote the Grimsby Evening Telegraph in its final edition of the day on August 21.

"She was still swimming strongly then and was almost certain to be the first woman ashore. Earlier she had been battling for this honour with Margaret Feather, of Scarborough, but at 2.45 there was no sign of Margaret. Earlier in the race, Brenda had been seized with cramp, but she carried on towards the shore – SINGING."

Throughout the long night, with only a watery, pale half-moon to illuminate the way, Brenda repeatedly sang Sing A Song Of Sixpence. The nursery rhyme may have seemed a strange choice for a grown woman, but there was reasoning behind it. Not only was it something to keep her mind occupied, the rhythm of the rhyme was perfectly in tune with her 25-a-minute swimming stroke.

Only once did she ask for help, and that was early in the morning when she asked the boat crew to put out their guiding light because it was shining on her goggles.

With Mr Mac in the support boat alongside young Grimsby swimmer Joyce Finch, whom Brenda had been training, she knew she had nothing to worry about. And as she walked up the pebbled English beach as the first woman to land, Brenda looked nothing but fit and fresh.

* * *

IT WAS TOUGH – She says
I WAS WORRIED – Trainer
SHE'S TOPS – Photographer

Brenda, who had conquered the Channel yet again, was making more headlines. Press coverage ran into many thousands of words in the days following Brenda's victory, as journalists around the world typed frantically to file copy. Radio bulletins buzzed with the news of a Briton's success, and cinema news reels spun madly into action to record the momentous occasion.

To Brenda, this reaction was somewhat astonishing. As far as she was concerned, she'd simply achieved another swimming goal, and that was that. But knowing how adverse she is to fame, this is unsurprising. She had found the attention during and following the 1951 race exhausting, and she was experiencing it all over again. At least, this time round, she knew exactly what to expect – even if it still raised her eyebrows with curiosity.

"Brenda Fisher swam further than any other competitor in the Channel race on Saturday," reported the Grimsby Evening Telegraph, one of her most staunch and loyal supporters. She had to – in order to take advantage of the course which crack pilot Jim Atkins had planned for her.

"So far away from the other swimmers did she go that Mr Billy Butlin's launch Britannia came up and trainer Herbert McNally and pilot Atkins were advised that they were 'taking her too far up'.

"This was the same warning Brenda's crew was given in 1951. Mr Atkin's reply was: 'I know' – two words which caused Britannia's crew to think that Brenda's pilot was crazy; two words which caused Pressmen, swim officials and spectators on the shore at Folkestone swim HQ to virtually rule the Grimsby girl out of the race. But Mr Atkins – and Brenda – knew what they were doing.

"That course brought Brenda in to land – the first woman across and the third in the whole race."

Now it was the turn of Evening Telegraph chief photographer Dennis Arnold to recount his experience. He was in the boat accompanying Brenda; in fact, Brenda wouldn't have wanted it any other way.

The local newspaper had supported her through and through, over the years. "The people in the accompanying boats were more worried than she was," recalled Dennis. "The rowing boat crew found it hard to keep going, she was swimming so strongly at the end… she would have sank before she gave up. It was tough going as she swam north away from the course of the other swimmers.

Brenda's welcome back to England

"Then it was easier through slack water to the twin lightships marking the Goodwin Sands. From there the tide virtually carried her, 'crabbing' down to St Margaret's Bay, but she had a difficult battle for about 200 yards across the strong tide before she landed on the beach."

As Brenda came within sight of the bay, Dennis recalled thousands of people cheering her on. "Just as she was cheered away from France," he said, "she was cheered into England."

Not, however, by officials, it turned out. The three Army men who had been the official observers in Brenda's two boats had to take a taxi into Folkestone and report her arrival - before the race officials realised she was out of the water.

"We were all much more worried than Brenda," said Dennis. "She was wearing a watch and several times called out: 'You are late with my feed, Mr Mac.'"

Afterwards, while Brenda was bathing at her hotel, Dennis went to the Folkestone swim HQ. There, experienced swimmers told him that Brenda must be, without doubt, the world's most stylish long distance swimmer. Dennis followed Brenda's progress every stroke of the way, and his photographs illustrate just how magnificent Brenda's Channel swims were.

He captured not only the important milestones, but smaller moments too, for example, when Mr Mac recovered a piece of timber floating in Brenda's path and when pleasure boats packed with supporters followed the final stages. Brenda swam through darkness and into the tidal current of the Kent coast to finish in a lively style, ready to pose for photographs and to say thank you to two holidaymakers from Newcastle who gave her a lift back to her hotel in their car.

Dennis was there when she told journalists: "I do not feel tired at all. I must get back to Folkestone to get ready for a dance tonight."

"She's terrific," Dennis concluded.

* * *

Later, she told journalists: "It was tough this time, but I was determined never to leave the water until I had finished. Though it was a harder crossing than in 1951, I came out of it without feeling any bad effects.

"I feel fit and well. The only thing that caused me any trouble was sunburn. Mr Mac seems to have suffered more than me. He felt unwell after the swim but is a little better.

"It's particularly thrilling to have beaten so many men in the race," she added, "but I knew that I had it in me to do it. The last time I swam the Channel I was horribly sick but this time it was grand all the way. I would not have left the water even if they had tried to drag me out. I did not feel the cold at all. I had hoped to make a better time but we met a strong head wind."

Mr Mac said: "How she swam those last two hours I don't know. It only convinces me that she's a miracle girl.

"After 12-and-a-half hours of swimming, she was 400 yards out but it took another two hours of slogging away to get in. I do not think any other person could have done it. I say conscientiously she is a miracle girl."

After completing such an arduous challenge, you'd think the golden girl would have retired to rest. Not Brenda. Donning a black nylon dress, she went out dancing with Joyce Finch but was back at her hotel by 10.30pm - not because she was tired but because she was too hot.

11

"We want Brenda. We want Brenda."

It was the evening of August 24, 1954, and Brenda Fisher, Grimsby's own Queen of the Channel, was coming home. And what a welcome the town planned to give her. Echoing the jubilant scenes of her 1951 homecoming, hundreds of people lined the streets, cheering and chanting until their voices became hoarse.

Many assembled hours before the train carrying Brenda was due. They jostled for the best vantage point, all determined to get a glimpse of the famous sporting blonde. Crowds gathered outside the town's railway station, in the Old Market Place and along the streets, ready to greet their heroine, some tightly grasping bunches of flowers, others using their elbows to push their way in. Women donned hats and their best coats, men were smart in suits and children were well turned out.

Brenda's arrival in Grimsby

There was no getting away from it. Brenda, the modest fisherman's daughter, was once again a bona fide celebrity - and her public needed her.

A newspaper headline the following morning screamed 'Grimsby welcomes its heroine home', and above the hullabaloo of the crowds, she told reporters: "This unexpected reception is harder to face than the swim."

This statement will sound familiar; it is exactly how she reacted three years before when faced with such adoration. Recalling the occasion of her triumphant return, Brenda simply chuckles.

"It was completely overwhelming," she admits, her eyebrows at once shooting up in surprise and immediately scrunching into a frown. "I had not really given much thought as to how people had reacted to the swim; I suppose it's because I was so focussed on doing the job in hand. Also, I'd already done this once before and I did not think people would feel that same level of interest.

"It sounds almost silly to say it but that is the truth. I simply did not think they would be interested as much. I was delighted at the achievement and knew people would be pleased, but I had absolutely no idea that they would react like that."

The excitement had reached fever pitch in Grimsby, and had spread to the surrounding area too. At Louth, the Lincolnshire market town some 15 miles away, a small crowd of well-wishers gathered at the train station to catch Brenda as she travelled through. They bought

Brenda with her trophy at the station in Grimsby

platform tickets and raced along as Brenda's train drew in. When they found her carriage, they besieged the door and kept her busy signing autographs while a steward in the dining car held up her trophy for all to see.

For someone who would rather talk about other things than herself, this attention was a jolt. The train journey had been comfortable and uneventful in the main. She was accompanied by Mr Mac and Joyce, and was looking forward to being greeted at the platform by her husband and parents. She had originally planned to slip home during the night, not to avoid well-wishers but simply to avoid a fuss. Grimsby could not – and would not - let that happen.

The day before her homecoming, Grimsby's Mayor, Alderman W Harris, declared: "There are 50 million people in this country and perhaps only half a dozen of them could swim the Channel and do a job of this sort. She showed great courage and endurance, especially in the early stages of the swim when she suffered from cramp. I think it is wonderful. The whole town is proud of her."

In typical Brenda style, she had little to say to the waiting reporters. The train pulled in at 7.40pm. Her attention was firmly focused on Pat, eagerly awaiting the return of his celebrated wife, and her mother and father. They were gathered with other relatives and friends, and stepping off the train, Brenda was overjoyed.

"I felt like I was going to burst with happiness when I saw them waiting for me," she recalls.

At the station entrance, a party of civic dignitaries greeted Brenda. The Mayor and his Mayoress wife, Deputy Mayor Councillor G H Atkinson and his wife, and the town clerk Mr L W Heeler and Mrs Heeler had words of congratulations for the swimmer. She was promptly presented with bouquets of flowers from the Mayoress, Mrs Harris, and Susanne Macklam.

The occasion was going by in a whirl of activity and before she knew it, Brenda was escorted into a car to begin her journey to Grimsby Town Hall. Standing on a seat with her head and shoulders through a sunroof, she held aloft the trophy she won for being the first woman across the Channel in the 1954 race.

The cheers of the crowds were "unbelievably loud", recalls Brenda. "They were waving and cheering, and shouting my name.

"As with the civic reception in 1951, it was one of the most surreal experiences of my life. The journey from the station to the town hall, in real time, should take about a minute. It felt like I was in the car for hours. I think it was then that it really struck me – that Grimsby was proud. And I was so proud in turn. I was very happy that day."

Among the crowds were 250 Grimsby schoolchildren, all members of the Central Recreation Club, who had cut short a picnic in the countryside to see their heroine.

At the town hall, Brenda was entertained in the Mayor's parlour. But she could not ignore for long the cries of "We want Brenda" echoing from outside. Wanting to share in her victory, people had gathered outside, so Brenda

Brenda arriving at the Town Hall

went onto the balcony to acknowledge cheers.

The Grimsby Evening Telegraph reported: "In a tribute to her, the Mayor said that in the streets they had seen enough to know that everybody in Grimsby was more than delighted and proud. They all shared the pride he was sure her family had in her magnificent effort." The Mayor spoke of Brenda's courage and determination of purpose, which, he said, was undoubtedly inherited from her mother and father.

"Mr Fisher was probably as good a representative of the finest type of fisherman as there was in the town," the newspaper report continued. "He suggested that it was that determination of Grimsby fishermen which had pulled her through."

Later, at home with her family, friends and Mr Mac, Brenda was tired but content. The Press could not resist a photo opportunity, however, and were pleased to obtain snaps of the happy domestic scene.

*　*　*

The following month, Brenda issued a challenge to three North American swimmers to a race in the Channel, or any other comparable distance in American waters. In truth, it was a stunt dreamed up by a publicity firm, keen to cash in on Brenda's fame – but she was willing to take them on, in any case.

The gauntlet was thrown – literally – to Marilyn Bell, Florence Chadwick and Winnie Roach, who were given the choice of time and place.

The challenge was made on Brenda's behalf in America by a representative of the Anderson Cairns agency, who actually had a white kid gauntlet made up with the words 'Brenda Fisher challenges' on a scroll. There was a minimum stake of £1,000, and the stunt was set up by Irene Cumming, an executive at the agency. Irene, a former swimming teacher, university graduate and newspaper woman, had moved to London from New Jersey, and would manage the challenge.

Marilyn Bell was the only one to respond. "I would not mind swimming against Miss Fisher," she said, "but I have to wait and see what they (Marilyn's agent) say. I have my heart set on attempting to swim the Juan de Fuca strait next but I also hope to try the Channel."

Following this statement, nothing else was heard from any of the three swimmers.

Brenda relaxing during training for Ontario

12

It was 1955, and with two successful Channel swims under her belt, she could not resist trying again – and this time, the massive stretch of water defeated Brenda Fisher. There had been confusion at the start of the race and she missed a tide mid-Channel.

She ended up being 45 minutes behind the other competitors because of the late arrival of her escort boat. And although she was allowed this in handicap time, she was forced to retire only three miles from Dover.

As usual, and not deterred, the Fisher girl's focus swiftly turned to Lake Ontario, in Canada. The mighty body of water was known for being unpredictable and exhausting.

The idea to cross a 32-mile stretch, from Youngstown to Exhibition Park, had been conceived the year before, when world-famous marathoner Florence Chadwick was challenged to swim it for $10,000. In fact, it was Toronto schoolgirl Marilyn Bell who made the headlines – by swimming it in 20 hours and 59 minutes, setting up a new women's world record.

Once the decision to go for it had been made, Brenda trained for sixteen weeks before travelling to Canada. She would swim for hours at a time in Cleethorpes Bathing Pool, under the watchful eye of her dedicated trainer and in full view of holidaymakers. Even trolley bus crews, whose vehicles were waiting at the terminus, watched on with interest.

She cut off her training early because it was "terribly cold for the time of year", and was soon preparing to head to Canada.

Brenda left Grimsby on June 17, wearing a green blazer bearing her home town's coat of arms, travelling by train with Mr Mac to London. She was waved off by her husband, parents and friends, and it was an emotional parting. In her luggage was a three foot long pennant, presented to her at the station by 15-year-old Wendy Carrington, the daughter of the owner of a

Cleethorpes amusement firm which had made the gift. Also stored safely was a box of chocolates presented by the Grimsby Cyclists' Club.

At Kings Cross, Jessie - who was at that time nursing in the south of England - was on the platform to greet her. From there, she flew to Canada from London Airport. Her luggage was 19lb overweight.

"I remember being excited when we flew over," says Brenda. "Pat stayed at home because he was playing football for Skegness, having left Grimsby Town FC at that time. It would have been nice if he'd been there but we both knew what our sporting commitments meant to each other. It was amazing visiting such beautiful places, particularly as a sporting champion; I had to pinch myself sometimes."

The party arrived via British Overseas Airways at Dorval, in south western Quebec, and the Press were hot on Brenda's high heels.

Mr Mac told local newspapers: "Her courage and stamina are remarkable. For training, we'll do anything from one mile to ten or more." He explained how her diet consisted of plain food, and avoiding sweets.

"I love chips but they are taboo while I am training," said Brenda, wistfully.

"We will find Lake Ontario water strange but will work up to it," Mr Mac added. "She's a good swimmer - I've never coached anyone else but the Fisher family since my own retirement from swimming - and I've never known Brenda to go making predictions she'll win, but she'll try awfully hard."

Mark Shaw, her Morecambe-based

Brenda going over the route with Mr Mac

manager from when Brenda Fisher Enterprise Ltd was formed, had suggested that she enter a lake race. Mr Shaw, gesturing with his cigar, told the local Canadian Press: "Without a doubt, I believe Brenda Fisher is the greatest long-distance swimmer in the world today. She has an almost blind and implicit faith in her trainer - and she is always willing to do everything he says."

And how would she prepare for hours in the water? Mr Mac told the journalists that she would be fed on snacks of tepid sugary tea, biscuits and sugar cubes. Brenda was using a mixture of olive oil and lanolin over her silk racing suit, he added.

Why olive oil, the reporters asked. "Can't tell you that," Mr Mac retorted. "Or else they'd soon all be using it."

*   *   *

The training regime in Canada was a tough one. Brenda was up at 6am every morning and straight into the waters of the lake from her bungalow as part of rigorous exercise. She would break for a light lunch and then return to the water in the afternoon.

"We stayed at a bungalow motel on the lakeside," she says. "I'd just walk straight out and into the water. The accommodation was gorgeous, and the weather equally so."

Her letters home were

Brenda arriving in Ontario

brief, for training came first; the swim, being in fresh water, was a harder pull than in the Channel, though not so long. Cross currents and high waves added to the less than ideal conditions.

She did have time for a reunion, however, and a most unusual one at that. When Brenda left school aged 15, one of the teachers was Florence Clark. Twelve years on, pupil and teacher met again - 3,000 miles away from home. Florence had moved to Canada and tracked Brenda down to her lakeside accomodation, in the appropriately named Humber Bay.

"It was such a surprise," Brenda says, smiling. "It was so nice to see a friendly face from my happy childhood. And that wasn't the end of it either; the reunions kept on coming!"

One day, the phone rang at her bungalow. She answered and on the end was the boy who used to deliver milk to her family home in Grimsby when she was a baby. Ron Cocking had immigrated to Canada, and was on holiday in Toronto when he read of Brenda's challenge and decided to track her down, just like Florence. Then, on her way to a TV appearance, someone stopped her in the street. It was a young man whom she had danced with some years before in Cleethorpes.

She also found the time to answer fan mail. Mrs A A Mills, of Freshney Street, Grimsby, was thrilled to receive a card from Brenda while she trained. It was in response to a poem Mrs Mills had penned about the champion swimmer:

Good wishes from Grimsby to Brenda,
And though she is far away.
We are with her thought and wishing her
Good luck and God speed on the way.
The courage she has is amazing,
And we know when she's put to the test,
We shall all have pleasure in knowing
That Brenda has given her best.

"I also found the time to visit Niagara Falls, a rodeo and a stock car match," she continues. "I went to a baseball match, where I was introduced to 12,000 people! And afterwards, I was presented with the ball as a souvenir. I was

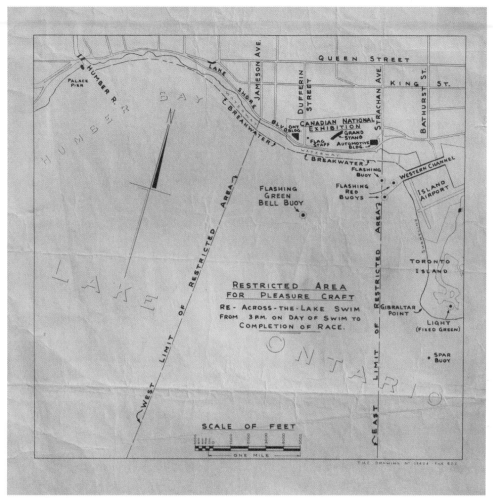

Map of Lake Ontario

treated very well by the Canadian people. They were very happy to host me, and I was very happy to be in such a beautiful country."

Bob Hesketh, a reporter with the Toronto Telegraph, visited Brenda at her bungalow. He wrote: "Brenda Fisher is built like a Channel swimmer and talks like Gracie Fields.

"Since she swam the Channel last year, Miss Fisher has been out of the water for two weeks. That was her reward for being a good girl. The rest of the time she has spent swimming about, her activities in the winter months being confined to swimming the length of a 19-yard pool which is only four feet deep at one end. That's the only bath that Grimsby, England, has although the town, undoubtedly proud of Miss Fisher, is in the process of building another one.

"Never having seen Miss Fisher swim a stroke, one would gather the impression that it is going to take a nasty lake to beat her. Miss Fisher isn't prone to talk much about herself, but she gives off an aura of confidence, almost stoicism, a characteristic one frequently finds in Englanders who are athletes, soldiers or statesmen. She admitted that the lake would be a formidable opponent but she said it in a way that left no doubt that she felt she could swim across it.

"Like when someone asked her what people got out of swimming across channels and things, for it must indeed be one of the toughest and usually most thankless forms of athletic endeavour.

"'Oooo well,' she said, like a lot of other Englanders would have said, 'It's got to be done, doesn't it?'"

The Press, once again, went crazy for the blonde from Grimsby. 'Channel swim is passé, Canadian dollar isn't, so Brenda to try lake' shouted a headline in The Globe and Mail.

She passed up an opportunity to swim the Channel again to take on Ontario, it reported. Her manager, Mark Shaw, said: "The Channel swim is on the way out. The training expenses are so high and the financial rewards so small, it just isn't worthwhile. That's why we entered the lake swim instead."

The ice-cold waters of the lake offered a tough challenge, but Brenda was well-placed for it. She would probably find it colder in fresh water than in salt, Mr Mac told the Press, but it was "just a matter of getting used to it".

Women, he said, made good swimmers because they are naturally buoyant, and swimming depends not so much on muscular strength as on technique. Brenda was inclined to agree. In an article she wrote herself for the local Press, she said: "A woman is better protected against the numbing cold of the water due to extra layers of fat and consequently she is not chilled to the bone as soon as a male competitor.

"This extra fat on a woman is very helpful over the kidneys. The kidneys are very vulnerable and are definitely a swimmer's weak spot. This is one attribute which lets women walk from the water at the end of the contest and give the crowd a cheery wave. Too often men stumble from the water showing distressing signs of strain and exhaustion."

She also revealed more about her intense training schedule. "Being a Channel swimmer, I quite often encounter this question: How do you train and why do you train that way? I can only answer this way every time. I train in a manner which my trainer thinks will give me the best possible chance in my swim. Herbert McNally is my trainer and I have been under his watchful eye for nineteen years. He looks for speed and endurance, and if he sees this he tests you over given distances and then teaches you how to gain speed and how to keep swimming for long stretches.

"Mr Mac took me completely under his wing and gradually instilled in me the mental attitude to train, train and train again. During those long hours of training, a close bond developed between us. Over the years of training, competition and success, this bond has grown deeper and become a great source of joy to both of us.

"During training, you have little incentive. Yes, there is always the goal in the distance but when you are training and training, you tend to lose sight of it. That's where the mental attitude I mentioned stands you in good stead. On the actual swim you have the incentive. During training… nothing but hard work.

"Gradually you draw nearer to the day of the swim. Two weeks before the event, Mr Mac will put me on a strict diet, then bring me to the peak of my performance, slacken it a bit, and repeat this until the event, when I should again be at my best. We will do a fair bit of distance work but of course we won't swim the course. Mr Mac and our pilot will make a test crossing to study the water conditions, currents and the like.

"The only time I will cross it, I hope, will be on the day of the swim and I should be swimming about 25 strokes per minute. We count one full cycle of the arms as one stroke. And it is during the swim that my mental attitude, physical condition and training will work hand in hand with stamina and some courage. As Mr Mac often tells me: 'You cannot be a good distance swimmer without the guts to have a crack at it'.

"And if you fail, your courage helps you smile and resolve to try again."

* * *

"And if you fail…"

That sentence was to prove somewhat prophetic, although not in the traditional sense of the word 'fail'. The Lake Ontario challenge date was August 13, during the Canadian National Exhibition's famous swim week. Grimsby's coat of arms was stitched proudly on Brenda's swimming costume and a flag, also bearing the town's signature boar heads, fluttered on her launch boat. The present record was 20 hours and 59 minutes, held by Canadian Marilyn Bell, who was the first to successfully cross it at the age of 16.

Brenda's mother told the Daily Mail: "The distance doesn't worry Brenda - she swam 52 miles to get round the Goodwin Sands in the Channel swim - but she has to get used to the different water. She's quite settled down and is very happy. Everyone is very kind to her, though she hasn't time to do anything except train."

Brenda was competing for £8,900 of prize money - or rather, $25,000 - offered by a Canadian soap firm, against about thirty other swimmers.

"But a lot of that goes on expenses," she was quoted as saying in the Press. "Fares and hotels, training and pilot's boat. Any prize money I got would be essentially spent on training and reinvested into my swimming. I won £1,000 in the Channel race in 1951, and out of that I paid Mr Mac and the pilot. Most of it just went straight back into my career."

The start of the race had already been put back twice within 24 hours because of strong winds had whipped up the chilly waters – waves were said to be ten feet high. Then came some bad news. The race was cancelled outright, to be replaced by a 32-mile swim along the Toronto seafront.

Six of the competitors made unsuccessful wildcat bids to cross the lake following the announcement, but Brenda made the decision to pull out and instead attempt a solo cross-lake swim when the weather improved.

She called off an attempt when winds reached 30mph, but did eventually take to the water. With sixteen miles to go, she was swimming strongly, even with five to seven foot waves slapping her in the face. She had completed two thirds of the course when her legs and arms gave out, and she was taken from the water. She was just nine miles from the finish line.

"I am very sorry folks," she told her supporters later. "I just couldn't make it. My legs gave out and then my arms." She had been in the water for 12 hours and 8 minutes, and had covered 23 miles.

And Mr Mac said: "You couldn't have asked a girl to take any more of that horrible beating. She just couldn't swim in any direction."

Back at home in Grimsby, the lights at Windyridge stayed on all night as Brenda's family waited anxiously for news. They were still waiting when the first rays of daylight crept across the sky, and only found out about the unsuccessful bid when a newspaper dropped on the doorstep.

Then the telephone rang. It was Mark Shaw's wife, with news. Her father said: "She must have packed up sometime late yesterday afternoon by our time. The message said that the weather had been very rough, Brenda had swum well and everything was OK. I know she will be disappointed but no one can fight such big waves for long."

*　*　*

Brenda quickly accepted an invitation to take part in the Lake Ontario crossing in 1956. She spent the following evening chatting and watching television with her friend and fellow competitor Gerda Olsson, from Scotland, who had also failed to make the crossing.

"It was one long tussle," she recalls. "The weather changed about five hours in and my pilot said it was the roughest water he had ever seen anyone swim in. We decided to try again in 1956, but in the summer, in an attempt to avoid the weather which literally brought us all to a standstill. Those waves were like a brick wall and Mr Mac's first concern was me, not the swim, so he made the decision to take me out.

"I knew I could do it though. I wasn't going to let it beat me."

Grimsby beckoned, but once again the weather had something to say first. The journey was delayed by a day because of Hurricane Ione causing havoc with flights. Brenda flew from New York, and was greeted by a welcoming party of Pat, her parents and Mr Mac's wife – but not before missing a train at Kings Cross because of the delay.

"I was very happy to be home," she says, "but full of hopes of returning. In fact, I left much of my swimming kit in Toronto in readiness for the next year!"

One thing she did leave with, however, was a lasting friendship with 19-year-old Gerda. "We were pals in the water and pals out of it. We ate and trained together, and would talk about the challenge. We knew we would be competing with each other but that didn't matter. We would just encourage each other. In the evenings we would relax, playing cards and writing letters home. By 9.30pm, we would be ready for bed, with a glass of milk. She was a lovely woman."

Tired, but feeling fit, Brenda was glad to be home in Grimsby. "At last!" she exclaimed, stepping over the threshold of Windyridge. "A good cup of tea!"

She had been away for three months, and had been drinking mostly milk. Although disappointed at the failure, she was more concerned with taking a rest for a few weeks, before going back into training.

Brenda wrote to a local newspaper in Ontario to thank residents for their kindness. "My gratitude to the people of Toronto, among whom I have had the pleasure of living. Due to their friendliness, I have never had a twinge

Brenda coming home with Pat and Mr Mac

of homesickness. I have acquainted my husband and parents with your city's kindness and they join me in thanking you all for your wonderful hospitality. I hope I shall be among you all sometime in the future."

* * *

"I challenge the world!" Aged 27, Brenda said she was ready to meet any of the world's best women swimmers in any part of the globe before 1958, when she planned to retire. "I am prepared to swim anywhere in the world but at the moment I have nothing definitely planned," she told reporters, after laying down the challenge.

Typically, Brenda could not ignore the call of the water for long, and set her sights on a marathon goal. She wanted to improve her leg stroke, so visited Wallasey especially to receive advice from Frank Parrington, husband of the former Olympic swimmer Lilian Preece. Although she had been swimming for years, she was always willing to learn more.

Each day she practised for a couple of hours and carried out other exercises. At one point, she took up skipping and club-swinging at a club run by Mrs Catherine Beasley, practising two times a week.

It was a determined Brenda who looked ahead to 1956, and the double victory it would bring.

Gathering in Egypt

13

Eyeing the warm, lapping water, Brenda Fisher's face was a picture of determination. She was in Egypt, and on April 6, 1956, she became the fastest woman to complete the 29-mile Nile River swim. By the time she left the cooler climes of England, accompanied by Mr Mac, she had been training for hours and had streamlined from twelve stone to ten.

Her mother told the Press: "The slimming will give Brenda extra speed in the warmer waters of the Nile."

Before departing, Brenda went to the Egyptian Embassy in London to meet General Dr M Sabry, who was president of The Long Distance Swimming Federation of Egypt. She sailed from Southampton on the liner El Malek Fouad, later returning on the same ship, which had been renamed Nafatiti.

On the first day aboard Brenda was seasick, as she is every time she sails. The boat stopped at Marseilles, Beirut, Genoa, Naples and docked in Alexandria, where she was greeted by the governor with a bouquet. And, of course, there was time for some sightseeing. Brenda took in the ruins of Pompeii and the volcano Stromboli, which was active both times they passed it.

She had been invited to take part in the race by The Long Distance Swimming Federation of Egypt, based in Cairo. The association wrote to Brenda in March of that year, welcoming her as an entrant.

The letter from General Secretary A F Shafshak read: "We like it very much to see you swimming in the Nile race, as it is expensive as you think we make it easy for you as such.

"We give you two return tickets on the steamer El Malek Fouad, sailing from Marseilles afternoon 21st March for you and the trainer. Your stay in Egypt and the trainer and other expenses are covered by us. So you see it is easy and I don't say it is a life's chance.

"General Dr Sabry is giving the press conference in the Egyptian Embassy in London on the morning of March 17, so you are meeting him there and getting your tickets from him."

The start of the race in Egypt

Not only was Brenda an international star, she was in demand in the swimming world. She was the only English competitor out of 37 men and women from 15 nations in what was the third ever Nile race.

It was sponsored by Cairo newspaper Al Gomhouria and it was open to amateurs and professionals, with prizes totalling £1,180 for the men and £827 for the women. The race was run in two stages; the first lap over 32 kilometres and the second, over 25 kilometres, the following day.

"The Nile race occurred in Egypt's summer, which was in April, and it was too hot for me," Brenda confesses. "It was a two-day swim and I got bad sunburn, which was painful. The sun would catch the back of me, and the right side of my face, as I would lift my head out of the water to breathe."

Thousands of locals gathered on the banks of the Nile at Helwan to watch the beginning of the race. The starting gun was fired at 7am by Lt-Col Hussein Shafei, the Minster of Social Affairs.

Not only did Brenda have to bear the blistering heat, there was a blinding sandstorm. The first lap was notable for the high number of withdrawals from sheer exhaustion. A strong south wind had whipped up the surface of the river into large waves, increasing the speed of the current.

"While this may have been advantageous on the down river section of the race," said one newspaper report, "it was a handicap that was not expected after the swimmers had turned the Gezira Island for the home stretch."

"We had a rowing boat to guide us, but the rowers couldn't speak English, so Mr Mac had a difficult time directing them," says Brenda. "The way the Egyptian competitors fed in the water was strange. They had sandwiches and even steak. I couldn't have managed that; my body would have rejected it. I would have felt too heavy to swim."

Of the women professionals, Brenda won the first lap, finishing in nine hours and nine minutes, and led for most of the race. But it was a close call. With only a few miles to go, New Zealand's Margaret Sweeney had a burst of energy and for a while, the two were neck and neck but Brenda managed to pull away, winning by one minute.

One newspaper report read: "There was nothing between them. They swam neck and neck, and a 'cat and mouse' game developed. Complications set in when, in their urge to gain the initiative, neither girl would stop to eat. Five hours passed before Brenda decided to risk it and stop for refreshment.

"It was the longest time in her swimming career that she had been without food or drink in the water. Luckily Margaret stopped simultaneously and after a few minutes, the race was on again. Brenda's victory by a minute was gained at the expense of having her face blistered by the scorching sun."

The following day, she won the second lap in three hours and one minute, again exactly sixty seconds ahead of Sweeney. The newspaper continued: "Brenda again beat her New Zealand counterpart in the shorter, final leg by a similar margin. Both beat the previous record by 90 minutes.

"As Brenda forged her way to victory, flowers were thrown into the water ahead of her by the excited crowd, who were shouting in English, 'Bravo Brenda!'"

Egyptian Hamed Mustafa, last year's winner, won both laps for the men professionals, and was the overall winner. Brenda was placed fourth overall.

At the celebration party back at her hotel, a large bottle of champagne came from the management and later at the prize-giving at a Cairo nightclub, she watched the waist-wiggling dancing girls with interest.

The front page of the Newcastle Journal gleefully proclaimed: "Brenda Fisher won the Nile international race for women professionals, with a narrow victory over Miss Margaret Sweeney, of New Zealand. Brenda beat her by one minute in the second and final lap of the race, finishing five and a half miles in three hours and one minute."

"Margaret finished about a minute behind me, so that was close," says Brenda. "I've swum with some talented people in my time, and made some very good friends. Margaret and I bonded over swimming and because of the unique situations we were in. It's good to have friends around you who have experienced the same things as you."

Mr Mac said the Nile race was Brenda's hardest swim ever because there was "no easing up".

There had been drama of an unexpected kind too. During the race, their Egyptian pilot went on strike. He did not speak English so they could not communicate, but Mr Mac had an answer. He threatened to kick the pilot into the river, which did the trick.

Before this incident, Brenda had been more than 100 yards ahead of Margaret Sweeney, but in the commotion, Sweeney forged on. Mr Mac said: "Brenda had to swim like the devil to catch up."

After the race, Margaret told them: "You were too strong for me. You seemed to get faster as the race went on."

"Races are won at the finish and not at the start," Mr Mac said, explaining that this is why he insisted on Brenda sprinting at the last stretch. "She is very easy to train. She always does as she is told and there's never a complaint from her."

* * *

"Miss Brenda Fisher has again put Grimsby in the news with her victory in the Nile swim and when she returns home, she will receive the congratulations of her many admirers," a local newspaper back home proclaimed.

"Anybody who knows Brenda likes her because of her modest bearing. Such success as she has achieved as a swimmer would have turned the head of some girls but Brenda has retained her old calm outlook, despite the fact that she is one of the best long distance swimmers in the world. Such skill, endurance and pluck as she has shown in her swims are admired by all and more particularly by those who live in this part of England.

"Her husband, Paddy Johnson, the Town FC player, must have been a proud man when, while playing at Mansfield on Saturday, he received a cable from his wife telling him of her victory in Egypt." He received the telegram from Cairo just before the match commenced. It read: "Good luck darling. Win today and let's make it a double victory."

She arrived home in Grimsby after a six-day journey by boat and train from Alexandria. All she wanted was a hot bath, a good sleep and something to eat. But Egypt had been good to her. Not only was she a winner, she saw the pyramids, the Sphinx, King Farouk's palace at Alexandria, a new experimental village which was being built in the middle of the desert and a huge textile factory, all the machinery for which had come from Manchester.

She took home a silver replica of the Nile Marathon Swim Cup, which took pride of place on the mantel piece at Windyridge, next to a bronze medal and an Egyptian banner.

It was safe to say that Egyptian cuisine did not hit the spot for Brenda and Mr Mac. "It was all goat," said Mr Mac. "Goat milk, goat cheese and goat meat. At the end, we all smelt like goats!" Incidentally, Mr Mac celebrated his 72nd birthday at a railway station at Marseilles on the way home to Grimsby. After a week's rest, Brenda was to go into training for a second attempt at Lake Ontario. But she and Pat still found time for a holiday, even if work was involved for one of the pair.

"The public baths in Dublin's fair city had a distinguished customer and many of the young Seans and Bridies were quick to recognise her," an Irish newspaper report said. "She was Grimsby's Brenda Fisher, on holiday in Ireland with her husband.

"Brenda's international aquatic achievements have not escaped notice, even in the Emerald Isle, as she was soon to discover. During their ten day stay, she was often approached in the streets and at the baths by eager Dubliners wanting to shake the hand of a world champion woman swimmer.

"In Dublin, they stayed with Paddy's father, sister and brother. The purpose of their visit was so that Grimsby Town's left half could take part in a representative game. Paddy played centre-half for an Irish International XI against an England XI. Ireland was beaten 5-4."

* * *

Three months after the Nile win, Brenda had yet to receive her £500 allocated prize money. It led to the Press Association asking: "Has Egypt – out of favour with the British people over the Suez Canal conflict – 'frozen the assets' of Brenda Fisher?"

Mother Fisher responded: "Brenda went to take part in the race at the invitation of the Egyptians, who agreed to pay the fare from Marseilles to Egypt on the understanding that Brenda would refund the money if she won. This has been deducted from her £500 winnings by the promoters, who also took 20 per cent (£100) as a donation to the Egyptian Distant Swimming Federation.

"Brenda's bank had been in constant touch with its Egyptian counterpart about the prize money but so far not a penny has been received. Last month Brenda received a letter from Margaret Sweeney, the New Zealand girl who came second, and said she had not received her money. As for the social side of her visit is concerned, there is no grumble whatsoever. Brenda and her manager were treated magnificently during the three weeks they were there but it does not seem fair that the prize money should not be forthcoming by now."

Mr Fisher added that the situation was a "damned shame". By now though, Brenda was back in Canada.

Brenda in her swimming costume at Lake Ontario

14

In a great battle of the elements in 1955, Brenda had spent three months at Lake Ontario for nothing. This time, the fair-haired secretary from Grimsby was steely in her resolution. This time, the lake would not beat her.

Invitations for her to take part in swims had come from Sweden, Italy, France and America, but it was Canada where she wanted to go. And on August 13, 1956, she crossed Lake Ontario.

Her time of 18 hours and 51 minutes broke the existing record by a staggering two hours and four minutes. It was the 41st attempt on the course in the last two years, and Brenda conquered it in black darkness and a terrifying storm.

With a freestyle rate of 52 strokes per minute, she started out on her solo swim at 10.45pm from Niagara-on-the-Lake on August 12, finishing at the eastern tip of Cherry Beach, Toronto, near the Dr Richard L Hearn coal-fired electrical-generating plant. Typical of Lake Ontario in the summer months, Brenda finished as a torrential thunderstorm engulfed the Toronto lake-front.

Only 54 people have been recorded as having completed the swim, and Brenda remains the only English swimmer on the list. By now, Mr Mac was over 70 and still acting as her coach. He was by her side, reported The Globe & Mail. As she waded ashore a winner, he remarked in his northern accent: "Ee, it's great. 'Tis 'n all."

* * *

She had returned, and had become a victor. 1955's failed attempt had fuelled Brenda to master the turbulent and unpredictable stretch of water. She flew from London Airport to Montreal, and then onto Ontario, carrying with her a doll mascot presented by Denise, John, Sidney and Sheila Mill, of Grimsby. There was a £10,500 prize at stake.

"I was very excited to do it," says Brenda. "I thought to myself, 'I'll show them what Britain is made of'. I was so determined to conquer it. It was cold water, but it was fresh, which is nicer if you end up getting a mouthful."

It was a solo effort, not a race, but four people entered the water that day to try it. The three others abandoned the challenge. Forty-year-old John Bass, from Ontario, gave up after about five miles, and Canadian Billy (Windmill) Connor, aged 20, was pulled from the water unconscious through cramp at 21 miles. Jim Edmunds also gave up.

Brenda says: "It was pitch black. I swam from Ontario, over to Youngstown and then followed Marilyn Bell's route. I was used to swimming in the dark, as we did that the second time I swam the Channel.

"I just followed the light on the rowing boat. But I didn't like it in the dark, and of course it was a lot colder in the water. You get a very acute sense of being alone, and it's very isolating. Mr Mac would never talk to me, but once he lit his pipe, I knew I was all right."

About an hour in, she started complaining about leaking goggles. "Mr Mac, let me take them off," she shouted. "These blinking glasses are horrible."

But Mr Mac ordered her to keep the goggles on. By 2.30am, her left eye was agitated and angry, and she stopped swimming. "I'm taking off these glasses and throwing them away," she declared, to the protest of her trainer.

She yanked them from her face and hurled them into the small boat. "I wish they went into the water," she said. "I'm throwing these things away."

Small exchanges like this show what it is really like being in the water for such a long time. How did Brenda cope with that isolation? "The dark does make you concentrate, which is a big part of distance swimming," she says, flicking through an album of photographs from the Ontario swim.

"That ability to be able to retreat inside yourself is really important. I used to sing songs in my head, Sing A Song Of Sixpence mainly, like in the Channel. It passed the time. You don't think about time, really. I would do between two and three hours before having my first feed, and then every hour after that. "Those feeds became benchmarks. I would have sugary tea, which I really hate actually, and bananas and chocolate. They are good because they give you energy, and they became like nectar.

"I can't remember dawn breaking. I was concentrating so much that all of a sudden, I realised it was daylight. Towards the end of the swim, there was a terrific storm, and it was rough. It was a hard landing. There were a good few people there watching, in their raincoats and umbrellas. They braved the storm to encourage me on. There were waves and a strong undertow. It's like a dragging feeling underneath you, but you don't really think about what's going on under the water.

"The coastguards were at the landing to guide us in. I remember approaching the shore and I could just about see the faces of the people watching. When you've done enough training, it just becomes natural and automatic to swim for that long, so there's no sense of relief at finishing, as such, more like a sense of achievement that I'd done it and it was ticked off my list."

Joyce Gibson, the daughter of Mr and Mrs C B Hebdon, of Grimsby, wrote a blow-by-blow account of the swim for supporters back home. Joyce, who

Aerial view of the Ontario race around dawn

had lived in Canada for two years and was a member of the Toronto Grimsby Society, described a tense atmosphere and a challenge which had attracted national attention. She recalled how the Canadian Broadcasting Corporation (CBC) kept up a running commentary of the attempt and relayed to Brenda in the water offers of prizes from individuals and companies should she finish.

"Sunday, 10.55pm," she wrote. "Brenda jumped into the choppy water, everyone is so excited. All eyes are on Brenda and offers of prizes are pouring in from all over the country, some from England too. Mr Cash, a Toronto jeweller, has just offered her a diamond worth $500 if she finishes.

"Monday, 2pm. Eight miles to go, Toronto in view and going strong. 2.30pm. Three and a half miles to go and growing excitement. She's going to do it and beat Marilyn Bell's record too.

"3.05pm. Three miles to go, $1,000 dollars given by an anonymous Toronto businessman, win or lose. 3.35pm. Two and a half miles to go but a strong wind has blown up and she's tiring. 4.05pm One and a quarter miles to go, water choppy. CBC commentators say that all Grimbarians should be really proud of Brenda.

"5pm Half a mile to go and going strongly doing 55 to 60 strokes a minute despite the weather. Very bad thunder and lightning, this must be the toughest half-mile of her career. Gifts are pouring in.

"5.30pm. Weather is awful. Wind gusts, teeming rain. Hundreds are lining the shoreline waiting for her, shouting and cheering. Aeroplanes are circling

The end of the swim

overhead despite the storm and photographers are jostling for position. She's done it and beaten the record!"

Brenda was welcomed ashore by Cherry Beach patrol officer Charles Hamilton (pictured).

"They drove me to the hotel, and I definitely had a good sleep that night!" adds Brenda. "The papers were full of the damage the storm had caused to properties and so on. I had not realised how nasty the weather had turned."

* * *

Brenda's feat was featured on the front page of the Toronto Daily Star but dominating the news was the devastating 10-minute freak storm. It had tragically claimed the life of 34-year-old Jane Carol Bradley, when a 4,000-volt hydro line crashed down in front of her home.

In the 'Home' edition of the newspaper, Brenda appeared under the headline 'Storm roars welcome as Brenda sets record', and provided a dramatic account of how Mother Nature greeted Brenda as she climbed ashore.

"Like the heroine of some Wagnerian opera," wrote reporter George Bryant, "Britain's Brenda Fisher was hurled onto an east end shore by lashing waves last night, the new champion of Lake Ontario swims. As she hit the shore, ironically a harbour commission dump area, the whole of nature, which had smiled on her during most of the swim, roared out as if in wrath at her victory.

"Thunder bellowed and seemed to shake the earth, lightning cracked across the skies, the rain sheeted down and the lake rose. Against this mighty backdrop, humanity did its best to do her homage. Sodden crowds lining the rain-lashed banks cheered, horns blew and whistles trilled. The recorded music of 'There'll Always Be An England' ground on and on from an escort boat.

"As Brenda came crouching out onto the shore, the world seemed to go mad. In front of her the crowd rushed forward. Above her, the sky cracked open and behind her, the waves climbed and crashed.

"People screamed and yelled, unheard in the tumult, lightning sizzled down at boats bobbing and milling in uncontrollable frenzy. And, like the quiet eye of a howling hurricane, Brenda, with typical British aplomb, walked with detachment in the midst of this cacophony. Hurtled forward by the waves, she waded towards shore until the water was only waist-deep, then touched the hand of a man on shore, symbolic of the land itself, calmly turned and walked out to her coach boat."

Mr Mac had crouched anxiously in the small coach boat, the Day Dream II, during the entire swim, and still had strength to stand and cheer when she waded ashore. Her only trouble throughout the entire swim had been a slight numbness in her fingers, but that had quickly passed.

"Perhaps it proves something about the beverage," the article continued, "or about the British, but Brenda stoked away many cups of tea as she crawled her way across the lake.

"With only 150 feet to go at 5.44, the clouds opened up and the deluge washed over the scene, blotting out boats, swimmers, shore and crowds. With 50 feet to go and Brenda, merely a storm-tossed bathing cap at this point, the visibility cleared slightly and the whole turbulent scene came into view. Her landing point was just east of Cherry Beach, a stretch littered with flotsam and jetsam. The thundering waves literally drove Brenda on to the shelf that projects out six feet from the waterline.

"Her knees bumped. Rising slightly on one leg, she reached out her hand to touch the out-stretched hand of a friend who had jumped into the water moments before to be in position for that dramatic moment. Helping her to her feet, he escorted her into a small mother-boat standing by, bobbing and tossing in the waves.

"From the boat, Brenda waved and shouted and threw a beaming smile at the crowds pressing about. In the main, Brenda's swim was undramatic. There were no tense moments or sudden weaknesses. The joyous pandemonium that prevailed at the swim's end equalled the now famous scenes of hysteria that greeted Marilyn Bell's shore-coming in 1954.

"The crowd at Cherry Beach, numbering in the hundreds, waded into the wild surf, shouting, cheering and brushing past soaking-wet policemen in an attempt to touch the radiantly happy English girl. The air, split by the cracks of lightning, resounded to the clamour of dozens of ships and car horns and marine sirens."

"It's the most fantastic thing I've ever seen," shouted CKFH announcer Ray Stancer from The Star yacht as the shoreline and water-borne crowds merged in the crashing surf.

Even mounds of muddy refuse and garbage forming a man-made barrier at the eastern point of Cherry Beach, caused by the storm, did not stop more than one thousand men, women and children turning out in support. In fact, the four-foot high mounds of refuse, which seeped an oily effluent into the surf, only served as vantage points for the throngs, as cameramen jumped into the dirty waves.

"The noise was tremendous," recalls Brenda. "I was still swimming when I could hear the cheers getting louder. Someone shouted 'Three cheers and a tiger!', and then the noise began to grow louder as I got even nearer. They were shouting 'Come on Brenda, come on Brenda'. It was an amazing feeling.

The Ontario finish

"It reached a frenzy when only a few yards remained and when I finally touched shore, there were literally screams of hurrahs, which were quickly drowned out by boat horns and whistles. That, combined with the thunder cracking overhead, was one of the most tremendous experiences of my life."

A tired yet smiling Mr Mac told reporters: "I'm very proud of Brenda. I am very proud to have trained the Queen of the English Channel, the Queen of the Nile and now the Queen of Lake Ontario."

And her first words, over the boat radio, were: "I feel fine thank you. I'll have my bath now."

After being warmed up and fed, Brenda arrived sitting in the front seat of an ambulance at the Royal York hotel in a yellow sweater and grey skirt, her platinum hair slightly tousled - the only indication she had just completed the gruelling swim. She took some food and drink. Wearing a yellow sweater and grey skirt, she waved to the crowd standing at the elevator. Smiling, she prepared to bed down for the night, literally dancing the way to her room.

* * *

As Brenda jumped into the water, one woman was right by her side. Grimbarian Kathleen Boyers was living in Toronto at the time, and Brenda says it was the support of Kathleen and Mr Mac that got her through the solo challenge.

Things hadn't gone smoothly when the party arrived in Canada. To their dismay, Brenda and Mr Mac discovered that Brenda's agent had secured no sponsorship, contrary to what they'd been led to believe. And the day before the swim, the pilot withdrew his services, despite a favourable weather report. Kathleen heard of Brenda's troubles and immediately telephoned the boatman. Together they made the journey to Niagara-on-the-Lake to test it out, hoping a bit of "Lincolnshire twang" might help raise morale.

During the swim, everything was going smoothly on the support boat. But a rather nervous reporter began getting on Kathleen's nerves. She could hear the exchanges between Brenda and Mr Mac, so when the journalist began pacing up and down, muttering "Everything's gone wrong; there is something wrong. It does not add up, I know something is wrong", she put a stop to it at once. Unable to restrain herself, Kathleen asked what the matter was. He replied: "I have been on all these swims up to date and there has always been pandemonium until tonight, and things have gone too peacefully for my peace of mind."

Kathleen set him on a more even keel by telling him that he was "dealing with a real champion and that he had better get some sleep before he conveyed any of his ill-bodings to anyone else."

Brenda was doing a steady 52 strokes to the minute when the weather turned, and people on Kathleen's support vessel became anxious. Then, Kathleen was the first to see the Toronto skyline – a happy sight for visibility was only four miles – and the finish was not too far off. At first the captain and the reporter thought it was Kathleen's imagination, but they soon agreed.

"In my excitement," she told the Grimsby Evening Telegraph, "I rushed to the rails and yelled, 'Mac, tell Brenda I can see Grimsby Dock Tower.'" It was the Canadian Bank of Commerce she could see, the tallest building in Toronto.

"Then the storm, which had hovered over for so long, suddenly burst with all its fury. It seemed as if Old Weatherman, who had held so many other swimmers at bay, was determined at all costs to stop Brenda. Lifeguards had been tailing her for more than an hour. Harbour police cruisers and yachts were surrounding her to try and shield her from the heavy waves which were crashing around her," Kathleen continued.

"As if in a final effort to stop her, the heavens opened wide, rain lashed down, thunder roared and lightning flashed across the sky, while a hundred-mile-an-hour gale tore across the city, uprooting trees, telephone poles, tearing off roofs and breaking windows. In the meantime, what of Brenda? Champion that she is, she too lashed out with a remarkable burst of speed, sixty six strokes to the minute, and within minutes was standing on the beach before hundreds of wildly cheering people, crazily enthusiastic for the English girl who had so gallantly braved and defied the elements in all their fury.

"Brenda was brought back on our boat after reaching the shore. I was waiting for her on the deck with her beach coat, with tears streaming down my face I wrapped the coat around her saying, 'I have a nice warm bath ready for you', to which she replied, 'That is just what I want but poor Mrs Boyers, you must be dead beat'. After swimming 32 miles in eighteen hours she still could think only of other people's welfare. A true champion in every sense of the word."

* * *

As she climbed out of the water after a record-breaking swim, Brenda's husband and parents back home in Windyridge were asleep and completely unaware of her victory. It was just after midnight when the telephone rang in Grimsby and a voice on the end of the line said: "Hello mum, I've done it!"

Brenda calling home to deliver the good news

She made the special trans-Atlantic call at about 6pm Canadian time.

Her mother told the Press: "There seemed to be a lot of excitement at the other end. By the sounds of it, a lot of people were singing and laughing. I am very pleased she has done it. She and Mr Mac were so disappointed when they had to retire last year.

"Since she returned home from that swim Brenda has worked hard for her success. She never missed a day's training; she even swam every day when she went for a short holiday in Ireland with Pat."

And here is how the call to Pat went: "Is that you Pat? Do you know why I have rung up? We went into the lake last night you know, and we've broken the record. We did it in eighteen hours and fifty-one minutes. I didn't wire because I know mummy worries when I am in the water. There was a storm at the end. It took quite a bit to finish."

Pat said: "It's the best piece of news I have had this year."

And Brenda's feelings? "It was a bit rough at the finish," she told her mother, mentioning nothing of the feet-high waves, lightning, thunder, torrential rain and gusty squalls that almost capsized the support boats more than once. The Toronto Telegraph crowned her 'The Lady of the Lake', devoting column upon column to the swim.

"The hardest time was the last few hours," Brenda told them, "although there was no time when I really felt defeated. The best thing of all was telephoning my husband."

The Canadian media were really taken with her. "On her visits here last year and this, she has shown a most pleasing personality… an outgoing nature demonstrated by her eagerness to help swimmers of less experience and fame. To the new Queen of the Lake, we say you're welcome in our neighbourhood any time."

Brenda had made the swim look almost easy, and Marilyn Bell – whose record time Brenda had beaten – was full of praise.

The Toronto Telegraph said: "Marilyn Bell is really glad Brenda Fisher got across. The girl who was first to swim Lake Ontario at 16 two years ago was an enthusiastic long-distance rooter for Brenda as the English challenger fought her way from Niagara to Toronto. The young marathoner has nothing but congratulations for Brenda on her clipping two hours and a bit from the time Marilyn made."

Marilyn commented: "Funny, it doesn't bother me about Brenda lowering my time. I knew it would happen sometime, and I'm glad Brenda is the one who did it, especially when she came from so far. It was a shame she didn't do it last year; her determination has really paid off.

"Brenda is a lovely girl. I've only met her once, last year, but she was very nice to me, very friendly and all that. So many people think so highly of her; she must be a fine person. I say, all the more power to anybody like Brenda. I tried to break her Channel record and I wasn't successful. Now she's broken mine, and I congratulate her."

After hearing the result, Marilyn sent Brenda a wire, which read: "It was a wonderful swim, Brenda. I'm very happy for you."

Even during the late stages of Brenda's swim, while she was still in the water, Marilyn sent a telegram which said: "Keep it up. You're terrific. I'm sure you'll make it now."

A fellow Canadian swimmer of Marilyn's, Cliff Lumsdon, was also warm in his praise of the girl from Grimsby. "Anybody who swims across Lake Ontario is quite some swimmer," he commented.

And Marilyn and Cliff's coach, Gus Ryder, said: "After missing last year, to come back and make a successful try is really tremendous."

Mr Mac, in his stoical way, was predicting great things. He told a journalist: "Brenda is now at her peak and barring accidents this may be her best year. She has wonderful pluck and stamina. She has got what it takes."

* * *

Brenda on the Ed Sullivan Show

Brenda woke up a couple of hours after dawn and took an early morning constitutional before breakfast through the hotel's corridors. For the most part, she went unrecognised among the tourists and hotel staff. Full of smiles and chatter, she looked like all she needed was another night's rest and off she'd go again across the lake.

Unwilling to be interviewed by waiting reporters until after breakfast, she said: "I feel fine. Just fine. After I've had a good breakfast, I'd like to talk about it. A good swim? Thanks, I did my very best."

In the days that followed, Brenda's star continued to rise, and she received an invitation to appear on the Ed Sullivan Show. "Ed drove me onto the stage in his car," she recalls. "I sat there thinking, 'Well, this is great!' It was in front of a live audience, but I wasn't nervous about it. He was ever so nice and very suave, and had a good sense of humour. Millions of people watched that TV show.

"I was in Canada for a fortnight in all, to do the swim and participate in the National Exhibition. But I stayed abroad for about five weeks in total, visiting New York and taking a boat around the Statue of Liberty.

"I went to many baseball matches and was a guest at a fair few dinners. In all of my swimming career, Canada was probably my favourite place. It was so clean and bright, not like New York, which was busy and dirty, like London. At the exhibition, I would do displays in the water and Mr Mac, on a microphone, would show the crowds how we were fed when we were

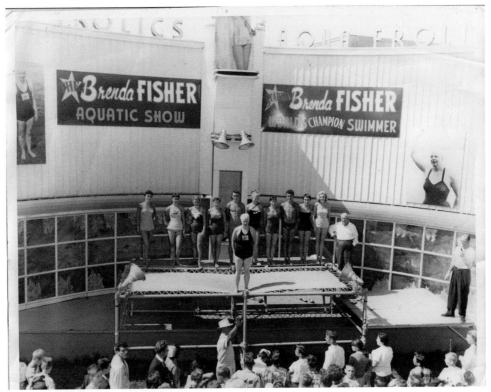

The Brenda Fisher Aquatic Show

on a microphone, would show the crowds how we were fed when we were swimming long distances.

"It was really cold because the pool was filled with tap water. We were there on Labour Day, and I must have repeated the display ten times or more. It was tiring, and I remember a steady stream of people watching... just a blur of faces, really."

Two Niagara-on-the-Lake firms had sponsored Brenda, but it was seven-year-old Teresa Rundle's monetary donation which made headlines in the Toronto Daily Star. The little girl, from Scarboro, had been given a gift of $7 by her uncle, but planned to give it to Brenda for completing the challenge. The girl called it "my greatest thrill" and had pestered her mother until she phoned the newspaper to ask how she could send the money. The gift was among many given by the local population as tokens of their pride.

Although her financial gain was little (Marilyn Bell received £26,700 in cash and gifts for her effort), Brenda was grateful. She received the freedom of Ontario at a special ceremony. She was given cash and merchandise of all kinds, including a $150 automatic gas hot water heater; one year's supply of Vel and Lustre Crème Shampoo; a two-year supply of sun tan lotion and one year's worth of soap, candles and sponges; half a dozen blouses; a chrome electric kettle; a year's supply of nylons from the National Nylon Co.; an orchid a week for six months from Jack Roberts florist; make-up; a $100 four-fur neckpiece; free hair dos for six months; a custom-tailored suit; a pair of tailored-to-measure slacks; and a male bird from The Budgie Shop.

The haul was worth about $1,000 in total, and Brenda had the issue of transporting it back home. Her mother told the Press: "I think Brenda is a bit worried about how she will go on getting all these gifts through Customs. We have been wondering about that ourselves, but we are all hoping she will manage it all right. I hope that the Customs officials remember that she received these gifts after doing something for her country."

But she would not mind if Brenda left one thing in Canada – the budgerigar. "We have one at home already," she said, "and I think one is quite enough."

Meanwhile, the town of Grimsby, in Ontario, sent red roses to "our Brenda" with a message of congratulations. They gave her and Mr Mac a civic reception, to which they were conveyed through the town by a pipe band. Later, a civic luncheon was held in honour of "the water nymph from Great Grimsby" at the Village Inn. During the evening, Brenda was presented with a walnut jewel case carved from an ancient local tree, on behalf of the citizens of Grimsby, and local organisations had raised a purse of money for her.

The locals, for a while, claimed Brenda as theirs.

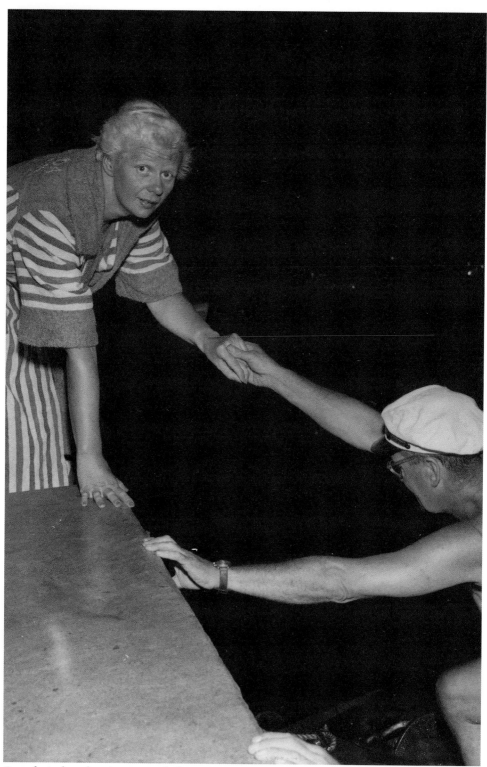

Brenda in her dressing gown, helping Mr Mac

15

"I knew I could do it, and I was determined to swim that lake," said Brenda. In a column written exclusively for the Toronto Telegram, she admitted: "There were a few bad moments, of course - right at the end - but that's when a good trainer comes through.

"Mr Mac has always trained me to swim better at the last than I did at the first. I have complete faith in him; he has it in me. I do what I'm told in the water. That's why I came out beating Marilyn Bell's record by two hours and four minutes. I don't mean to sound as if I'm bragging – I'm not. I have a wonderful coach. He never lies to me – about time, about distance or about anything.

"I get so worried about Mr Mac, there in the small boat. I don't mind if it rains, but it worries me to death to see him there, out in the wet without a mackintosh. It happened during the swim – I had to laugh. It was in the morning, when I was feeling a little dismal there, swimming all alone. It would rain a few drops. Mr Mac would put on his Mackintosh. It would stop – he would take it off.

"It gave me quite a lift to see this little comedy in the middle of the lake. As soon as Mr Mac took off his coat, the rain would start. It didn't bother me at all, until the very last, when the rain began to fall so heavily that the folk aboard the accompanying boats began to disappear below deck.

"That is, all but the Day Dream II crew. They were there all night, even when it was lonely, and even in the rain they were there all where I could see them just at the last.

"I was seasick last year – the waves were so high – but this year I was fine all the way along. I was a bit seasick on the way home, mind you. The ambulance ride from the dock to the Royal York Hotel upset me a little. But once I was in the suite arranged for me by The Telegram, I felt right at home.

"But to get back to the swim. I'll admit I'm a bit of a fussy eater – I didn't like the oranges much. But I did do everything that Mr Mac told me to – and that's why I got across in the time I did.

"I've got to thank my old friend, Kathleen Boyer, for my food. She prepared most of it and she was always on the job. She even kept showing me my mascot dolls – I've got three from my friends in Grimsby, England, my home town.

"You know, I've never had pacers in a swim before. But a nice young lad, Ken Greig, jumped in with me in the late afternoon and stayed with me for a good four or five hours. Then later on, Ted Simmons paced me until almost the end. They were both wonderful. I hadn't met either one of them before but I think of them now as very good friends.

"It's a very lonely business, this swimming the lake. I heard Mr Mac telling reporters that, and I agreed wholeheartedly – although I didn't take the time to say so. The night was lonely. If it hadn't been for the voices aboard the Day Dream II cheering me on, I'd have been lost. The worst time was really the last few hours, although there was no time when I really felt defeated.

Brenda greeting the media on her return from Ontario

"I had a lovely bath aboard the Day Dream II when I came out of the water. Mrs Boyer rubbed me down, and I never felt better. I've always been able to walk away from a marathon swim, and I was glad that I could walk out of Lake Ontario. I wasn't really surprised when Dr M A Simurda, who examined me after the swim, told me that I was in top condition and that I could swim again today if I wanted. I felt good.

"So here I am – second woman to swim Lake Ontario. Now, I don't know what to do next."

* * *

Brenda arrived at Grimsby Town Station on the 7.50pm train from London. When she stepped off the train with Mr Mac onto platform two, there was a small group of family and friends waiting for her. Very few people knew she was coming home.

"We wanted it to be a quiet homecoming this time," said husband Pat. He'd had a shock earlier when, being first to board the train, he walked through all the corridors to find his wife apparently absent from the compartments. He was starting to think she hadn't caught the train on time when he found her, in the last compartment but one.

Brenda, dressed in tweed and a rust-coloured pillbox hat, said: "I've really enjoyed being in Canada but it's good to be home."

Her many gifts from the Canadian people were following her by boat; the only thing she carried with her on the train was a black toy poodle mascot. Among the first to greet Grimsby's world champion was Jack Jewitt, chairman of Grimsby Cyclists Club, who was also caretaker of the baths where Brenda trained. Also waiting to welcome her were three small children, Sheila, Sidney and John, who, in all of her recent swims, had seen her off at the station.

Not all members of Brenda's reception party were on the platform. As the group passed over the footbridge, a small man in a raincoat was waiting near the bookstall.

"It's dad!" said Brenda, and ran to hug the former Grimsby skipper. She was home. With Brenda's feet firmly on British soil, rounds of public engagements followed.

She started an inter-departmental freestyle team race for the WP Appleyard Cup swim at the Orwell Street Baths. She visited an exhibition of radio, television and electrical equipment by Fred W Wood Ltd at Grimsby Town Hall and tried out new radio headphones. The headphones, which had been designed by Mr Wood, were being given to patients by the League of Friends of Grimsby Hospital.

She then let a hairdresser loose on her famous blonde locks when she became a model for Mr R Wilson, who was giving tips on hairdressing to members of the Cleethorpes company of the St John Ambulance brigade at their autumn fair in St Peter's Church Hall. And she was special guest at a dance held at the Winter Gardens to mark the end of the working holiday season at Wonderland, the amusement arcade on Cleethorpes seafront. Spot prizes for dancers ranged from toilet seats to eggs, and they were entertained by colleagues who put on cabaret spots. But Brenda was the star attraction alongside her husband.

At a civic reception in her honour, the Mayor of Grimsby, Alderman Matt Quinn, said: "I would say that this has probably been the toughest of all of her swims, and the Canadians recognised it as such. Brenda and her party have been advertising Grimsby and its fish all over Canada."

He didn't think her swim had been given much national publicity, adding: "I don't want her to feel the town doesn't think much about it. The people of Grimsby were talking about her success all of the time."

But Brenda was delighted with Grimsby's response. "People were coming up to me in the street," she says, looking back. "They were very excited for me, and pleased that I'd achieved something else for Grimsby to be proud of."

So what was next on the swimming horizon for our blonde-haired lass? She was asked if she would consider swimming the 18.3-mile strait of Juan de Fuca, separating Vancouver Island from the mainland. It is considered by long-distance swimmers as one of the most treacherous in the world. Only recently, Marilyn Bell – the first woman to swim Ontario – had withdrawn through sheer exhaustion just five miles from the shoreline.

"I will swim anything – if it's made worthwhile," was Brenda's response. Time marched on to 1957, and then the issue of payment for the Nile race raised its head. More than a year after the challenge, Brenda's cheque was in her hand, but it would still be a month before it was cleared by the International Bank.

She then told the International Long Distance Swimming Association, who wanted her to swim in a Capri-to-Naples race, that she was not interested. Brenda was, by now, back in a routine of life at home in Grimsby. She was on the office staff of Ross Group Ltd, still training though with plans to complete three swims in Mexico, Vancouver and Ontario. She was also planning to take on the Juan de Fuca strait if a sponsor could be found.

* * *

In 1957, Brenda still held the women's world record for the Channel, and it was her ambition to cross the English Channel once more before she left competitive professional swimming behind for good. She once again plunged into an intense training regime. At Eleanor Street Baths, she was watched over not only by Mr Mac, but Rex, a golden retriever. He became her training mascot, and belonged to the caretaker, Jack Jewitt.

Dogged Brenda was eyeing the £1,900 prize when she made the journey to France, and it was simply tradition when, 24 hours before she was due to swim, the race was postponed because of six-foot high waves. In what was her fourth and last attempt, after nine hours in the water and suffering from sea sickness, she was forced to retire – just five miles from the Dover coast.

To make matters worse, her record was beaten by one hour and 42 minutes by Greta Anderson, who finished in eleven hours – only 10 minutes outside the overall record which was set up in 1950.

Billy Butlin, who again sponsored the race, donned a bathing costume and jumped into the water to swim the last 40 yards to shore with Greta. Brenda, aged 30, was overcome by seasickness after battling for more than nine hours against a strong north east wind, rough sea and mist. She was piloted by Jim Atkins in his boat Golden Harvest, and he had to help her from the sea.

Later Brenda was driven by car to the headquarters set up for the race. Jim's wife told the Grimsby Evening Telegraph: "My husband found it very difficult to steer the boat across. He told me the wind was very strong and they kept running into swirling mist.

"He had no other alternative than to lift Brenda out of the sea. She was very sick and even after reaching the bay had not fully recovered. My husband is in bed now. He doesn't look so good and he has made several Channel trips."

There were 38 swimmers in the race, representing 19 countries. Brenda had been training hard since January, with only a week of training in open water due to bad weather.

* * *

Brenda Fisher retired, aged 31, from professional competitive swimming as the fastest Briton, man or woman, to swim the Channel from France to England. For the last eight years, she had spent eight months of every one training daily.

No longer would she be forced to get up at 7am for a programme of exercise until the evening – unless she wanted to.

Her retirement from sport in 1958 came not long after she participated in a swim from Capri to Naples, and suffered bad sunburn. She spent eight hours and thirty minutes in the water for the 21-mile swim. The blazing sun sent the thermometer up to 109 degrees and the water up to 78 degrees. It was so hot that she had to retire even though the coast was in sight.

About 10 of the 28 entrants finished the course, all but the winner being carried from the water in stretchers. "The combined effect of salty water made me sick so often that I could not make progress," she recalls. "It was just awful."

That year also saw another landmark occur in Brenda's life; Albert Fisher, her beloved father, died at his home. By now, he had been retired from fishing due to ill health. He was 69, and had died from the combined effects of asthma, heart failure and chronic bronchitis.

"It was a strange time," Brenda admits. "Dad dying was a bitter blow, and taking the decision to retire from swimming was hard. "The competitive swimming naturally came to an end. I knew I'd had enough. Mr Mac was getting on as well. To be honest, it was all I'd ever known, and not having it was very hard to get used to at first.

"Time lay heavy on my hands, and I never liked housework. Mother urged me to go into work, so I joined Ross Group as a sales representative, where I spent many happy years. I also went into teaching swimming at the Mermaids club."

Brenda and her dad

Her employment at one of the world's largest frozen fish firms kept her busy, working alongside Pat, where he joined after giving up football.

Suddenly, she chuckles loudly. "When I retired, I was like a child in a sweet shop when it came to food! I ate whatever I wanted, but then I put too much weight on and had to diet anyway! To this day, I absolutely adore chips. It was also great to have freedom. One of the first things I wanted to do was go to London and visit Madame Tussaud's, and go to Petticoat Lane on a Sunday morning."

Once people realised she was on the market, in a manner of speaking, the blonde bombshell of the briny found herself in great demand. She became a technical advisor for a committee which was making plans for a cross-the-Wash swim between Skegness and Hunstanton.

There were 10 entrants for the first race, on July 14, eyeing a prize of £175. But it was called off because of bad weather; three swimmers carried on for 30 minutes before they realised. All along she was encouraged by Mr Mac, who was pleased to see her enormous talents being transferred to others.

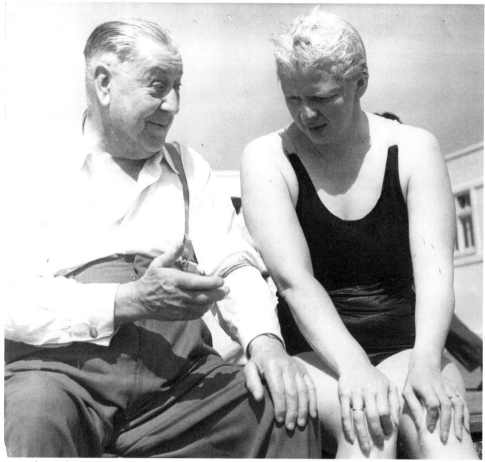

Brenda with Mr Mac

The man who made a champion out of Brenda died in June 1961, aged 77. Wherever she went in the search for trophies or titles, he was by her side.

He was there when she swam Morecambe Bay as a teenager, and when seven foot waves tossed her in the waters of Lake Ontario. Brenda was naturally devastated.

"I owe it all to Mr Mac," she says, her eyes softening. "I could not have done any of it without him. He had been ill for a week and was admitted to Scartho Hospital. I was upset for some time, but so proud to have been taken on by him. He had become a friend as well as a coach, but he remained strict with me right until the end. Mother always used to say he was the only one I'd obey or listen to! No one could replace him. If I had decided to carry on swimming, I would have managed myself.

"I wouldn't have wanted my husband or any of my family in the small boat accompanying me on swims - it would have been too hard on all of us. We had such a lovely friendship, and I will always be grateful to Mr Mac for being an absolute inspiration."

* * *

If Brenda thought her fame would wear off, she was very wrong.
The 1960s saw many more public appearances, a duty which she has continued through the decades to the current day. She fondly remembers swimming the first length of a new swimming pool in Grimsby in 1962.

The £288,000 pool not too far away from Windyridge was officially opened by Lord Luke of Pavenham, who had shown photographs to the Duke of Edinburgh, who, in turn, said it looked "quite magnificent". It took Brenda 25 seconds to swim the inaugural length when the pool was opened before 600 guests. As she walked to the edge in a red costume and white cap, she was given a standing ovation lasting more than a minute. Then, she plunged into the water to swim two lengths, and was given a presentation box of chocolates by the lord.

Later, she returned to the pool – to win a £5 bet. The challenge arose through a joke made by former Grimsby skipper Bunny Newton, who at that time owned a bingo hall. Bunny donated a trophy to the Santa Marina swimming club, and challenged Brenda to race a length. Bunny said: "I do not think I have got much of a chance but Brenda's a marvellous lass. She might even slow down a bit for me!"

Brenda, now 44, took it on and arrived on the agreed date to find that Bunny could not make it. She swam the length alone, swimming under ASA laws, and won the bet.

* * *

For four decades, the Grimsby Santa Marina Club promoted competitive swimming in the area. Brenda, one of the founding members, ran a Saturday morning babies class, teaching very young swimmers up to a bronze level before they could join the club as full members.

The club was formed in 1969 and the name was derived from Santa Clara, a very successful Californian swimming club in the 1960s, while Marina reflected the fishing and marine history of Grimsby. Swimming in the area had tapered off somewhat, so a group of like-minded people got together to do something about it.

Brenda, Ray Tindall, June Marshall, Tom Gristwood, Alex Kirten, George Penrose and Cooper Turner were determined to make things change. Peter Prestbury was, at the time, one of England's top swimming coaches. The group approached him, and it was his appointment that led to the club's formation. It was the first in the country to employ a professional coach.

Schools had a training scheme in operation, which was run by Grimsby Dolphins swimming club coach and teacher Tom Pecket, and the children involved in this became the very first members of Santa Marina. In its first year of formation, the club achieved eighth place in the then Motor Way League, latterly the Speedo League. At one point, the entire county team was made up of only Santa Marina swimmers. Before the club's closure in 2010, Brenda would return to present trophies.

"I am proud to have been involved in it," she says. "It was so well-known in Grimsby and around the region, and it was an honour to be involved and help so many younger people."

Brenda presenting a certificate

16

For a woman so well known around the world, Brenda is relatively unaware of her fame. Search for her name on the internet and you will find scores of results. Old press photographs of her various swims are available to buy on auction websites, and yet it simply passes her by.

"I don't think anything of it," she says, smiling gently and shaking her head. "I still get stopped when I go out shopping, which is lovely. It is nice that people remember, particularly locally, but I've never really thought about that side of things."

Jessie and Buster swiming in Alexandra Dock

Brenda is so unassuming; it is difficult to draw her on the subject. She has countless personal appearances under her belt, numbering into the hundreds, from schools and clubs to national events, such as the Royal Command Performance.

"Doing things like the Command Performance just seemed to happen; generally, I would get a telegram or would be contacted directly, I was told where to go and I turned up. I certainly didn't have a public relations manager or anything like that. I don't think it works like that these days!

"I met a lot of celebrities, including the actor Bill Boyd, who played Hopalong Cassidy on the television, at a reception at Butlin's in Skegness. I also remember going on the BBC radio show Younger Generation, to talk about my career. Much of it was going to local events though. I went to Laceby British Legion's sports and baby show after the 1951 swim, where I won a live pig and a large iced cake!

"I hated talking in front of groups of people. I just didn't like it, and still don't now really. If I was invited to something like that, I'd take Jessie with me and make her do all the talking. I very much kept myself to myself in that regard."

One appearance where she unavoidably had to be herself - and herself alone - was on the popular radio TV series, Calling All Forces. Among Brenda's carefully preserved archives is a script, bearing her name alongside a roll call of Bob Monkhouse and Ted Ray. It is signed by the cast.

Having been pre-recorded the day before, the episode aired on October 7, 1951 to the nation. To the sound of Geraldo and his Concert Orchestra playing Entry Of The Gladiators, Brenda was introduced by Ted Ray as "a charming young woman who recently distinguished herself by swimming the English Channel in record time".

"Well, Brenda," he continued. "I don't suppose you're aware that I too am a very keen swimmer. In fact, only this afternoon I went for a dip in the local baths."

"Oh, I know Ted," Brenda replied.

"You do?"

"Yes, as I came into the theatre, I heard the two commissionaires talking, and one of them said Ted Ray is all wet!"

The jokes continue for three pages; to be expected in a finely crafted script from the pen of Bob Monkhouse, naturally.

"The radio show was very good fun," recalls Brenda, "just like lots of the things I did. I can't tell you how many events I went to. For some years, I advertised 7-Up and travelled all over. When I was in London for them, I used to stay at a flat in Mayfair and would get my hair done at the famous Teasie Weasie salon. It was great!"

Ellen Joyce, the Tasmanian keyboard virtuoso, confessed that Brenda was her heroine. She had always wanted to swim the Channel but a back injury meant she could not swim. And Brenda met royalty of another kind, the king himself – Elvis Presley. It was while she was in Canada, on the many rounds of publicity she carried out.

"I was introduced to him," she recalls. "He was very nice and very handsome, and a real gentleman. I was just another person he was introduced to, but I was thrilled."

At home in Grimsby, the costume Brenda wore for the 1951 swim made 30 shillings when it was auctioned by the Grimsby Cyclists' Club.

It, and one of the suits Brenda trained in, was won by Mrs N Newman, of Dover Street. The money went to the King Terrace Boys' Club's Fund For Old People and the Eleanor Street Old People's Home. She was a household name, so it was no surprise that the advertising industry wanted a slice of Brenda's fame, too.

It was Quaker Oats, the cereal famously known for giving energy, which Brenda became the face of… in an unusual way. The firm used a photograph of Brenda as a very young child, with the tagline "Who is she?"

"She learnt to swim in Cleethorpes," the newspaper advert read. "By the time she was 20, in 1948, she had swum Morecambe Bay in two hours, 37 minutes - breaking a 34-year-old record. Blue-eyed and fair, she held the Mermaids Swimming Club backstroke, breast stroke and freestyle championships. In 1951, she swam the Channel in 12 hours, 42 minutes - the fastest time ever by any woman. You're right - it's Brenda Fisher!"

"I can't afford to miss my breakfast of delicious Quaker Oats," Brenda proclaimed in the copy. "I need the energy it gives, and Quaker Oats makes a useful contribution of Vitamin B, the vitamin we all need, every day."

Now, she says: "Yes! I definitely do like Quaker Oats. I used to eat it a lot, but now I have Shredded Wheat or toast."

Brenda's Quaker Oats advert

Brenda also appeared in the August 30, 1951 edition of society magazine The Lady. In the Noted In Town column was a picture of Brenda, with Jessie on her arm, being escorted by a smart-looking policeman into Grimsby Town Hall for a civic reception.

At home, Brenda lit a miniature Olympic flame on top of the Savoy Cinema at a party to mark the 75th anniversary of the Grimsby News. She held the torch aloft in a striking pose to mark the town's premiere of the Technicolor film of The Glory Of Sport. She reached the roof by climbing a perpendicular ladder into the attic of the cinema, crawling through a skylight and onto the roof in heavy rain and darkness, accompanied by cinema manager Mr H B Goodman, and a

Grimsby News photographer. He got his picture by standing with one foot on the slippery slates of the roof and the other on the ledge overlooking Victoria Street.

And getting the flame itself to the roof was no mean feat. A cylinder of acetylene was manhandled up and hauled by ropes to be fixed to beams. "Excuse me, but I think the top of your cinema is on fire," said a small boy to the doorman, as the pelting rain eased.

Brenda was one of a party of 45 of Grimsby's future sporting athletes, who were entertained by a showing of the film. Frequently referred to as the Grimsby blonde, Brenda is thought of with great affection by her fellow Grimbarians.

Brenda's friend, swimmer Joyce Carroll-Stenton, said it was a privilege to be in the support boat when Brenda swam the Channel in 1954. In a letter to a local newspaper, she said: "It was an experience I shall never forget. We went across in a small boat to France where Brenda started and after swimming all night and into the next day she finished as fresh as she started – a truly wonderful swim.

"I had already swum Morecambe Bay and the Humber and had done a few other short swims, but was never good enough for the Channel having seen it! Brenda and I trained together in Eleanor Street Baths every Saturday morning, 500 lengths of the pool, and in Grimsby Docks. Brenda was and still is a very remarkable lady who put Grimsby on the map."

Resident Ken Barr, in an edition of the Grimsby Evening Telegraph's Bygones supplement, wrote of the 1951 swim: "I was in the Army and was visiting a cinema in Salisbury when this story came on the news.

"I let out a loud cry of triumph which, in a quiet cinema, didn't go unnoticed. The next thing I knew, a torch was being shone on me and the usherette's voice saying: 'Will you come with me please?' As I was being escorted to the manager's office, I thought I was in trouble. It turned out quite differently. The beaming-faced manager told me that he came from the Grimsby area. He apologised for not having anything stronger and gave me – and my mate – a free ice cream."

And this from another unnamed resident: "We all put up decorations in Hope Street for Brenda Fisher after her Channel swim. A group of lads found an old metal fire kerb and for some reason were banging it with sticks as she was driven past – anything to make a noise."

On an internet forum, EF posted: "When I was a young lad in the 1950s the name Brenda Fisher was spoken in highly respectful tones. The daughter of a Grimsby fisherman, 'our Brenda' swam from France to England, setting the then fastest time for a female to conquer swimming's Everest.

"An accomplished marathon swimmer, she also became the third person ever to swim Lake Ontario in 1956. In her honour, the fine people of Grimsby bestowed on her the local equivalent to a Hollywood Oscar by naming a tug after her."

* * *

Grimsby has a reputation for producing great sportsmen and women. The former sports editor of the Grimsby Evening Telegraph, Geoff Ford, wrote: "In fact, it is virtually the only thing that has kept the town in the national headlines over the years. From Channel swimmer Brenda Fisher and Wimbledon tennis player Shirley Bloomer in the Fifties, through to bowls star Amy Monkhouse (Gowshall) in the 21st century, our sports stars have carved their names with pride.

"The Eighties and Nineties were the eras of snooker, golf and motor cycling. Professionals Mike Hallett and Dean Reynolds were, at one time, rated six and seven in the world and both won the English Professional Championship. Hallett reached the Benson and Hedges Masters final where he lost to Stephen Hendry. They both stood on the shoulders of previous giants, the most notable of which was Ray Edmonds, the world amateur champion.

"In motor cycling, Roger Marshall and Roger Burnett burned it with the best. Marshall was several times British Champion while Burnett was a star of the Grand Prix circuit.

"Golfers from the Grimsby area have won European titles. Stephen Bennett took the Tunisian Open while Jim Payne was victorious in both the Italian and Balearic Opens. Grimsby has hundreds of martial arts devotees and much of the credit for the spread of the sport is down to Sharon Rendle. The girl from Grimsby Judo Club reached the very top at the Seoul Olympics in 1988. She became the first person from the town to win a gold medal.

"On the track, the Colebrook sisters, Jane and Katrina, competed with the best over the middle distances and Jane brought home an 800m silver medal in the European Indoor Championships."

Grimsby, indeed, has a proud sporting tradition and its list of triumphs continues to grow; providing not only inspiration, but pride. Little did Brenda Fisher know that she was a particular inspiration to one young chap still in short trousers, who would go on to be known far and wide as the Humber King.

* * *

Ten-year-old Pete Winchester bounded home from school, ran into the house and made a beeline for the radio. Twiddling the dial, he tuned in to the news bulletin, jigging around until he heard the words he'd been waiting for: "Brenda Fisher".

"In the days of my youth, people didn't have a lot of money, so my friends and I would go swimming in the tide every single night," he said. "I lived for it, and it became what I waited for at the end of the day. If I misbehaved, my father would simply ban me from going swimming, and that was awful.

"Harry Jackson, my swimming teacher at Eleanor Street school, was a so-and-so. He would make us go in the water even if you couldn't as much as float. I think if you can swim, then you've really achieved something."

"I was a child when Brenda first swam the Channel," he continued. "At that time, there were some fantastic swimmers in Grimsby. When she was actually swimming the Channel, I would beg my dad to keep replacing the accumulator on the radio so I could listen to the reports. Dad was twiddling the dials, and we were so excited that we could hear reports of Brenda swimming.

"I also remember asking dad for threepence to go to the Rialto Cinema, in

Grimsby, to watch the Pathe news reels of her achievement. It was great seeing it in the national and international news; Brenda well and truly put Grimsby on the map.

"I used to live down Hope Street and everyone living along the street was sports crazy. My dad came home from work at lunchtime shouting, 'She's in the water! Brenda's swimming!' So I ran in the house and tuned in the radio.

"When my dad came home from work that night, he said, 'She's landed – she's swam the Channel.' Even then, I knew what the Channel was and I was ecstatic. Listening to the radio and watching Brenda on the news planted the seed in my mind. I knew from that moment that one day, I would swim the Channel just like Brenda."

Pete only began swimming so he could play football. His father told him he had to swim or he would not be allowed to join the school team.

"I am thankful for that now," he said. "Otherwise I wouldn't have discovered something I love so much. Funnily enough, I have peanuts to thank too for getting better at swimming. I used to dive under the peanut barges which

Brenda and Pete

docked in Grimsby and come up the other side. The workers on the barges would throw peanuts to us kids. If you couldn't swim, you didn't get peanuts."

Football, peanuts and Brenda combined to drive Pete to be the swimmer he is today, the holder of his own records. No one has swum across the River Humber from Spurn Point to Cleethorpes more than Pete, who has crossed it 70 times since 1975 – a world record. His quickest time is two hours and ten minutes and his slowest is a gruelling five hours and 47 minutes.

His nearest rival was Tony Espin, who has done it around 28 times. Tony, who was on the committee of the Channel Swimming Association, trained Pete with swims of up to five miles in Alexandra Dock. Pete's inspiration was, of course, a certain Miss Fisher.

He said: "When I was young, I used to say I would love to swim the Humber. "To be fair, it was my lifetime ambition. After the first time I could not wait to do it again. In fact, I did it the following week! After my first two swims somebody suggested I try and do five. Then it went up to 10 and so it has gone on. I had every intention of stopping at 21! I have swum all over the place, but the River Humber is my favourite."

He has swum the length of Lake Windermere and was only foiled in his solo attempt to swim the Channel in 1979 by painfully slipping not one but two discs in his back.

He recalled: "There was a radio station on the support boat who phoned my dad on loudspeaker. I was so close to the end that my dad said he was going to open a bottle so I punched the air in celebration - and slipped two discs."

But the Channel did not beat him in the end. He crossed it as the lead swimmer of a relay team in 1986. Pete is also the only man to have ever swum from Hessle Foreshore to the Grimsby Dock basin – the equivalent of a marathon. He is also a familiar figure at Grimsby Docks every Christmas Day and New Year, taking a dip in the icy waters as part of the long-held tradition in the town.

In 1968, the coldest year Pete can remember, the docks were frozen solid for 13 weeks. On Christmas Day, when most were cossetted up against the cold, he punched a hole in the ice with a pick axe and jumped into the -2°C water.

He said he has "only ever once been cold while swimming", during a Humber crossing in 1975 when he was taken to hospital with hypothermia.

Piping engineer Pete, who has raised thousands of pounds for charity over the years and met the Queen Mother, says he would not have achieved what he has without the support of his wife Vera, and son Gary. In 2002, he announced his retirement from swimming, but the draw of the water proved too strong; he was back in the Humber in 2003, completing his 66th crossing. It was the best conditions he'd had since 1975.

As in other crossings, Pete was visited by a seal which was nosing around and also had close encounters with big ships in the estuary. "I just couldn't resist," he admitted. "I had to keep going." And he kept going all right – until he gave up for good on what was his 70th crossing.

But he has shared his gift, by helping more than 150 other swimmers cross the Humber over the years. He is a much-respected trainer. "Swimming is my life," said Pete, a member of Grimsby Water Rats and chairman of the Grimsby and District Swimming Association. "That feeling when you touch the bottom and you've completed the swim is out of this world."

Nowadays, Pete is proud to count Brenda as a close personal friend – something his young self would ever have dreamed of. It came about because of his friendship with Brenda's husband.

Pete said: "I played table tennis with Paddy after Grimsby Town had finished training. He was brilliant. By that time I was really into my swimming and I saw Brenda at the swimming baths all the time. I always made sure she knew who I was. Then as the years went on, we became good friends through the local swimming scene.

"When I decided I wanted to swim the Channel, I went to Brenda for help. She spent hours with me, rowing in the boat while I swam. It was brilliant. He added: "Her story is fantastic and she is my heroine.

"Brenda and her generation were the pioneers of long distance swimming – they just did it without knowing what we know now. I will not let people forget Brenda, and what she has done for swimming and for Grimsby."

In early 2015, Pete was awarded an MBE for his achievements.

* * *

Michael Read, president of the Channel Swimming Association, is proud to call Brenda a friend. The association is the governing body of Channel swimming, regulating crossings, ensuring they are officially observed, and keeping swimmers safe.

Born in Brighton, Michael took up swimming at 14 and joined the association in 1969, making his first crossing that year. He still competes internationally.

Michael said: "A Channel swim is and always will be a battle of one small, lone swimmer against the sometimes savage vastness of the open sea. It is quite possible to be ten miles from shore on a pitch-black, cold night, with a cresting sea, a three-knot tidal stream and thirty metres of depth underneath… in such conditions, the Channel is no place for a physical weakling."

In July 2009, the Olympic swimming veteran swam the Humber, after being cajoled into the idea by his friend, Humber King Pete Winchester. But there was one condition – that Michael was introduced to Brenda.

"Today, as was the case 65 years ago, not every swimmer chooses to register their swim with the CSA, but Brenda Fisher did and so we were fortunate to be able to observe her swim and verify and ratify her swim," he explained.

"Her first Channel swim was delayed by bad weather for 36 hours; it is hard to imagine the stress that that must have put her under. When the race finally got under way she was accompanied on her swim by a rowing boat and two oarsmen, and for food she was fuelled by a little chocolate and sugar.

"Again, it is easy to forget that these items were still on ration, our sugar allowance was just 65g a day and sweets just 15g a day. To provide the 10,000 calories she would need for a swim of this nature she would in theory have required more than 2000g of sugar - someone's sugar allowance for a month. "She was in fact only the 10th woman to swim the English Channel from France to England when she walked ashore, as bright as a daisy, after 12 hours and 42 minutes.

"She had just won the second ever Daily Mail Channel race in a new ladies record time. She had just competed in an international field of the world's greatest swimmers. Not only had she beaten all the ladies, but after 12 hours, she was only 30 minutes behind the winning man.

"Brenda Fisher is not a name that rings many bells today but it should. Her name was on every tongue and she was the toast not only of Grimsby, but of the whole nation. When she returned home from her incredible English Channel swim from France to England it was to a well-deserved tickertape welcome, a Civic reception and a crowd of 20,000 well-wishers.

"Today, with all the technology available at our fingertips, with motorboats, mobile phones, sports drinks and maltodextrin carbohydrates, improved materials for bathing costumes, detailed weather forecasting and computer power, perhaps 50 swimmers or so worldwide, swim the English Channel each year, a miniscule number compared with those who climb Mount Everest.

"We can quite clearly conclude that they were pioneering days and that Brenda was very much a pioneer."

Brenda and her dog, present day

17

Brenda is that pleasant kind of shy. If her achievements are mentioned, she looks down into her lap, or bats the words away with her hands. This trait is very endearing to all who meet her.

Now she is particular about what events she attends, not because she isn't interested, but because it can be rather demanding. And when she does make a rare public appearance, she is normally accompanied. Instead, friends, fellow swimmers and admirers tell the stories for her, and she is perfectly happy with things that way.

Sitting in her comfortable living room with her faithful dog by her side and an unfinished jigsaw demanding attention, it is easy to see why. Her achievements are different now; she's immensely proud of her family and she loves her friends dearly. She is also a cancer survivor.

After swimming and the whirlwind which came in its wake, she enjoyed a working life. She left the employ of Arthur Drewry to run the sweet shop with Pat, before giving that up to move to the Ross Group in 1962, where she worked for more than 25 years.

Nowadays, in her retirement, she enjoys keeping up-to-date with sporting matters and likes to hear what's happening in and around where she lives. She, of course, became - and still very much is - a celebrity in Lincolnshire, and remains an ambassador for swimming.

"I had the opportunity many a time to move away, but I never really considered it," she says. "Even when I was married, we lived here, in the house I was born in and the house I live in today. I must be Grimsby through and through!"

"It is quite strange that my life, particularly when I was aged in my 20s, was so closely scrutinised swimming wise," she reflects. "Even my marriage was of interest to the media, and all those people waiting outside the church just to catch a glimpse…" She breaks off to shake her head in disbelief before resuming. "I was just a woman who happened to be successful. I think that with training and genuine dedication, anyone could tackle the English Channel.

"I'm not saying they would do it quickly, but if they really wanted to, they could probably get to the other side. I was always shy and never really had a driving ambition to swim the Channel at first, but I just thought 'why not'.

"If I hadn't have got into swimming, I honestly don't know what I would have done or what would have become of me. My whole life has been swimming and everything has revolved around it. I think it was my destiny.

"Everything has been for the sport, and it's unfeasible to think of my life without it. I wouldn't have seen half of the places I have, and for that I'm grateful. I would have just been here in Grimsby, I think.

"We visited Grimsby in Ontario, where I was presented with a tray, which I still have. I kept almost everything but I only have one cup now, which is the Festival of Britain trophy. I loaned the rest to the Santa Marina swimming club, which I helped set up.

"I still try and keep fit and do as much charity work as I can. I enjoy going to bingo and socialising with my friends, but I do love sitting at home with my dog and doing jigsaws. Pat had no patience for that sort of thing!"

She adds: "I watch the television and see people swimming the Channel now in about six hours these days. It is just unbelievable. Swimming was wonderful for me. It was never about the prize money or the records. It was just about the joy of doing it."

Brenda Fisher will forever be the woman that brought Channel glory and worldwide sporting fame to Grimsby. In doing so, our modest, shy blonde in deep water has created an inspirational legacy which will outlive us all. Brenda, Grimsby's Queen of the Channel, we salute you.

Brenda, present day, reflecting on her swimming career.

Author's Note

Writing this book has been as thrilling for me, as a journalist, as walking ashore after swimming the Channel must have been for Brenda Fisher. Time has not lessened the fever-pitch excitement her achievements brought to Lincolnshire.

A black and white photograph of 20,000 people gazing up at the balcony of Grimsby Town Hall, waiting for their heroine to make an appearance, is powerful and moving. Being Brenda at that moment – and knowing how shy she is – must have been overwhelming.

There are many people who deserve thanks for their help in bringing Blonde In Deep Water to life.

Veteran swimmer Peter Winchester has been instrumental, in that it would not have been written had he not suggested it. I thank the Winchester family for their unerring patience.

I also want to thank my family for their love and endless cups of tea. Grimsby Telegraph archivist Linda Roberts, deputy editor Michelle Hurst and journalist Peter Chapman have been inspirational in their support. And thank-you to editor Michelle Lalor, who has given permission for the use of scores of articles and photographs. The Telegraph was with Brenda for every milestone of her career, and sometimes every mile she swam.

My final, and most vital, thank-you is reserved for Brenda. She has endured hours of questioning and trusted me with custody of her precious archive. Most of all, she has trusted me with her story, for which I am very honoured. It has been a privilege and I too am proud to call Grimsby's Queen of the Channel a dear friend.

Lucy Wood
http://lucywoodauthor.com

Notes